46710

WELSH BROTH

BY

THOMAS JONES, C.H.

The world is much larger than England, isn't it?
I'll never be just English or just Welsh again.

ALUN LEWIS
In the Green Tree.

India Command
April 7th, 1943

W. GRIFFITHS & Co.
4, CECIL COURT, LONDON, W.C. 2

46710

β

Made and Printed in Great Britain
by the Cambrian News, (Aberystwyth), Ltd.

TO THE STUDENTS OF THE
UNIVERSITY COLLEGE OF WALES, ABERYSTWYTH
AND THE STUDENTS OF COLEG HARLECH
FROM THEIR PRESIDENT

PREFACE

IN *Rhymney Memories*, published in 1938, I tried to describe a boy's life in a Welsh mining village in the eighteen-seventies and I followed this up in *Leeks and Daffodils* (1942) with some account of student life in a Welsh college in the nineties. I now add some chapters of my subsequent life in Scotland and Ireland and back again in Wales before I settle down, in middle age, in England and start another story.

It will be at once clear to the reader that in these random recollections I am attempting neither systematic autobiography nor intimate self-analysis but am primarily interested in my friends, in acknowledging my debts to them, and in providing the social historian with a few footnotes. Whole tracts of experience are omitted, high streets and by-streets, lanes and footpaths. Little is said of my secretarial and administrative lives which properly belong to my second forty years. In these pages I am a student, a college lecturer, and for a single session a full-gowned professor.

In writing I have had in mind the students to whom I have ventured to dedicate the book. I desire to thank one of them, Mr. Aneurin Davies of Rhymney, for preparing the index of names.

T.J.

Aberystwyth
Christmas 1950

CONTENTS

Photo by]   [H. Evered Davies, Aberystwyth

THE UNIVERSITY COLLEGE OF WALES, ABERYSTWYTH

WELSH BROTH

MY decision to leave Aberystwyth and continue my studies elesewhere had been taken. I was what would be called today a mature matriculant, that is, a rather elderly student whose schooling had been interrupted, in my case by wage earning for six years, in industry. I had since spent five sessions at college and achieved the summit of a student's ambition in becoming vice-president of the Literary and Debating Society, but this eminence only made more conspicuous my repeated failure to pass the Intermediate examination of the University of London. The charm of Mathematics eluded me ; it was a closed room to which I had not the key. One person after another commiserated with me and made me feel discouraged and disgraced. Ought I to go back to timekeeping at the steel works in Rhymney ? I would be branded a ' failed B.A.' for the rest of my life. I must leave Aberystwyth. Oxford and Cambridge were beyond my reach scholastically and financially. Should I give up the quest for a degree and betake myself to a theological college ? That would be a surrender which would distress my father and mother to whom the possession of a degree was the one proof of academic success which they understood. The thought of continued dependence on them was galling, yet they never questioned my decisions nor withheld the small supplies within their reach.

What had I gained by my stay at Aberystwyth ? My dominant interest had been religion and its practical application to social conditions in South Wales. I had moved from evangelicalism to the study of social questions ; from Liberalism to Labour ; from the theology of the Pauline Epistles to the economics of the Kingdom of God. I was earnest and enthusiastic, ascetic and nonconformist. My ambition was to be dedicated to a life of unselfishness in the service of the poor and unprivileged.

I had read text-books and books innumerable and in doing so had been gripped by powerful personalities, of whom Mazzini was the chief, and to his message I responded in some measure and helped to spread it. Of the sciences, biology for example, I knew nothing. Like Juvenal, I had never examined the entrails of a frog. (Sat. III. 44). Perhaps if I had I might have known my own body and controlled it better.

I had mingled with many students, younger and older than myself, and this contact and collision of minds and sharpening of wits enriched my experience and enlarged my outlook. Amongst them had been several women students of shining character and high intelligence, one of whom I was, to my great surprise, presently to marry. U.C.W. did much to train pioneers of the higher education of women. These women were more important in my life than were the men. They were variously attractive and resistant ; intellectually they were hardly inferior to the distinguished group of men students—Tom Ellis, Ellis Griffiths, Samuel Evans—who a little earlier had achieved prominence in Wales as members of Parliament. The women came most of them from England. One of them, Annie M. Dobell, in January 1895, became head of the Girls Intermediate School at Blaenau Ffestiniog, and then at Pontypool, and a member of the College Councils at Cardiff and Aberystwyth. She had a Welsh mother. " Honour, anger, valour, fire," it was said, had been given her at her birth. I recall also Beatrice Edgell, Phoebe Sheavyn, Beatrice Ewart, Alice Jackson, Sophie Bryant—

they passed on to adorn the teaching world or to conceal their identity in marriage. Man does not fall in love with brains, but with other qualities ; in my choice of Eirene Lloyd brains were associated with beauty and goodness, in combination a dazzling trinity.

Then there were the Professors. Great teachers are always scarce and this was true at Aberystwyth. When I look back I recall three outstanding men on the staff : Thomas Charles Edwards, the first principal, of whom I have written elsewhere[1] : Thomas Francis Roberts, the second principal ;[2] and C. H. Herford, the Professor of English.[2] The two principals were primarily Greek scholars. The one was charged with quickening scholarship and with passionate spiritual energy which made the old texts come alive ; the second had the same power to a less intense degree— he took longer to ignite : he lacked the geniality which puts a student quickly at his ease ; his influence was due to a transparent interest in your welfare in this world and the next. The Professor was a scholar and critic endowed with a nimble intelligence and a mastery of language which was itself a kind of eloquence. Herford is described in the *Dictionary of National Biography* as " the most accomplished English scholar of his age." His asthmatic delivery lessened his control of the rougher element in his class and such was their superfluity of naughtiness that on occasion the Principal had to be brought to the classroom, where he sat through the lecture and secured perfect order. All three teachers possessed the extra quality which transforms knowledge into inspiration and far tran- scends the demands of university examiners. They were sharply contrasted with the industrious pedagogues who found the chief attraction of Latin, Greek and English in their grammatical peculiarities.

[1] *Theme and Variations.* P. 126.
[2] *Leeks and Daffodils.* P. 29, 36.

At what point I first came to think of the University of Glasgow as a port of refuge, I cannot at this distance of years remember. In such major decisions there are untraceable elements, secret indescribable perceptions which gradually gather precision and determine the course of our lives. Glasgow was large and anonymous and I could hide my examinational shame in its fog. At Aberystwyth I knew everybody—we were few enough for that to be true. I had exhausted the virtues of that experience and having always more curiosity about men than powers of concentration on books, I was entangled in innumerable time-wasting and unprofitable acquaintanceships from which it would be a relief to escape.

There was, moreover, in Glasgow, a powerful magnet which drew me. Henry Jones was now settled in Edward Caird's Chair of Moral Philosophy. Jones had been a young schoolmaster who had been helped from Wales to Glasgow by a scholarship provided by a forgotten Welshman, Daniel Williams, born in the seventeenth century.

Williams came from the Wrexham area and rose beyond ' a vulgar pitch ' by a great natural vigour of mind. At 21 he was chaplain to an Irish countess. After spending twenty years in Ireland he settled in London as a Presbyterian preacher and polemical leader of nonconformity, counting Richard Baxter and Daniel Defoe among his friends. Defoe has left among his writings *Memoirs of the Life and Eminent Conduct of that Learned and Reverend Divine, Dr. Daniel Williams.* Williams was a considerable scholar but he was not so bookish, says his earliest biographer, as not to mind how the world went, nor, I may add, was he so immersed in theological controversy as to fail to marry in succession and after a decent interval two heiresses of distinguished piety and great wealth. It is true he kept a coach, and smoked a pipe, but on the whole he must have lived frugally and carefully and husbanded his fortunes—unlike his eloquent Welsh assistant, John Evans, who also married a rich widow, but despite the excellence and popularity of his sermons on the duties of the Christian life, lost her money and his own in the South Sea Company. Both prudent pastor and poor assistant share the same vault in Bunhill Fields.

When Williams died childless in 1716 he left about £50,000. He made a will running into forty printed pages octavo, and arranged for its administration by twenty-three trustees.

Various bequests provided for the teaching of poor Welsh children to read English, for the preaching of the Word of God in Wales, for the relief of aged and poor ministers, the assistance of widows, the distribution of books and, almost as an afterthought, the maintenance of a library. Out of this testament came the well-known school for girls at Dolgelley, which preserves the founder's name ; assistance to the Presbyterian College at Carmarthen; the Dr. Williams Library in Gordon Square, London, and much besides.

A special interest in the Scottish Universities led Williams to found scholarships to enable ' South Britons ' to go to Glasgow. In the eighteen nineties they were of the value of £40 per annum and had been held by several young men who were later to become prominent in our Welsh life. My fellow lodger at Aberystwyth, R. R. Williams, and I went together to London to sit for these scholarships, being examined in Greek, Latin and Mathematics. He won and I failed. He went to Glasgow and I tried again but the scholarship went to Robert S. Franks, later to be a learned theologian, whose son, Sir Oliver Franks, I was to meet in 1947 as a Pilgrim Trustee before he went to Washington as British Ambassador.

So without a scholarship, I joined R.R. in lodgings in Clarendon Street, Partick, where for a session we shared a concealed bed or shelf in a cupboard opening off our sitting-room,

The good that has followed in the wake of Daniel Williams justifies this brief record of his benevolence. He counted on being both useful and famous after his death and to that end he arranged for the periodical reprinting of his own booklet, " Vanity of Childhood and Youth", for the term of two thousand years. He did not foresee that the collection of his books would grow into the splendid library in University Hall, Gordon Square, and be of far more value than his own pamphleteering. In accordance with the Founder's provision for the holding of Quarterly Meetings I dined with his Trustees in October 1946 at the Library and celebrated a grant of £2,000 made by the Pilgrim Trustees to enable a new catalogue of the Library to be prepared.

I write these lines in another library, St. Deiniol's, Hawarden, a few miles from the birthplace of Williams, founded by Mr. Gladstone, " for the effective promotion of Divine learning " and before me lies Mr. Gladstone's copy of *The Presbyterian Fund and Dr. Daniel Williams's Trust* published in 1885, marked in the margin by Mr. Gladstone. It was in October 1895 that Mr. Gladstone drew up a preliminary paper with a view to the formation of his Trust. It is therefore certain that before his death in 1898 he had studied the history of the earlier Trust while contemplating his own bequest and foundation.

When Daniel Williams was paving the road to knowledge for Welsh youth in 1716, Scotland was newly united to South Britain by the Act of 1707. Glasgow was a small fishing town on the Clyde exporting herrings to Brittany, but it was already renowned for " pleasantness of site, sweetness of air and delightfulness of its gardens and orchards ", " somewhat like unto Oxford " wrote John Ray in 1662. The Clyde had always been important. Pre-reformation bishops drew their salaries in part from its salmon ; later, the indentures of weavers' apprentices contained a clause limiting their diet of salmon to three times a week for their protection against having too much. When I went to Glasgow in 1895 it was the

Second City of the Empire.   Tobacco, coal, iron, steel, a river, and
hard work had wrought the change.   The Clyde was crowded with
ships and mariners.   Nearly a million men, women, and children
were housed in high and massive blocks of stone tenements, " ruled
into pigeon holes," coated with carbonic deposits, formidable and
forbidding structures, as unhomelike to a southerner as could be
imagined, distributed over an undulating site of low hills on the
banks of the Clyde and the Kelvin.   The heraldic motto of the city
was ' Let Glasgow flourish ' abbreviated from a much older and
longer original inscribed on a bell ordered to be made for the Tron
church in 1631 : " Lord, let Glasgow flourish through the preaching
of Thy Word and praising Thy Name."

When I think of an appropriate modern emblem I call to mind
a figure by the Belgian sculptor, Constantin Meunier, of a tall,
powerful blacksmith, in leather apron, leaning on the shaft of a
mighty hammer.   Whereas others were born with silver spoons in
their mouths the makers of modern Glasgow were born, like the
Napiers, with hammers in their hands, though it must be conceded
that it was the Incorporation of Hammermen who denied James Watt
the use of a workshop in which to carry out his experiments.   Never-
theless marine engineers found their way into thousands of steam-
ships, big and small, which travelled to all parts of the world, pro-
claiming the reliable workmanship of the cooperating Clyde artisans.
" The clang of their hammers mingled with the professor's voice as
you sat on the class-room benches.   Through the windows you
saw the smoking chimneys of factory and foundry under the
engineering skies."*

The ten to twelve hours journey between my home in Rhymney
and my lodging in Glasgow was always made via Crewe and usually
by night.   Crewe is not a terminus but an intermediate state.   Many

* Smart, *Second Thoughts of an Economist, xxxv.*

a purgatorial midnight hour I spent in its station awaiting the train from London, half awake, half asleep, in deep discomfort on its hard benches, or stamping and shivering along its platforms loaded with mail bags and parcels and crates of new bicycles from the midland factories.   I tried to puzzle out the crossword traffic, up, down and across, which took overnight a letter from one village to another, miles apart, and the train of thought would be interrupted by a load of somnolent coaches, blacked-out ghostly sleepers, pulling up from Euston bound for Holyhead or Perth and Aberdeen.   At last I boarded the Glasgow train to the annoyance of the settled slumbering passengers.   At Carlisle I would show in turn the same resentment to an intruder.   I once heard Sir George Adam Smith say that had Christ been our contemporary he would have placed the parable of the Good Samaritan not on the road to Jericho but in a railway train. At Carlisle locomotives were changed and the thick husky hooter told us that we had reached the Border.

Emerging from the Central Station at six o'clock on an October morning I encountered at once Glasgow's stern solidity through the grey dawn.   I boarded a tram and trundled over the granite cause-ways to my gloomy lodging.   I remember noticing that the smooth sandstone surface of the tenements was chalked over with the hieroglyphics of passing schoolchildren so far as their little arms could reach.

Clarendon Street, Partick, was no different from a thousand other streets but it had the advantage of being reasonably near Gilmorehill, the site of the university palace built by George Gilbert Scott in 1870.   For two hundred years the Old College had been in the east end, off the High Street, in the neighbourhood of the Cathedral and the Cross, where it housed some four hundred students.   Until well on into the eighteenth century lectures were delivered in Latin, and into the nineties of the nineteenth, professors sat at the receipt of custom and collected the students' fees in golden sovereigns ; class prizes were awarded by the votes of students. The large income from students' fees and the long vacations made the Scottish Chairs among the most attractive in the Kingdom. There survives in Andrew Lang's *Life of Lockhart* (I. 78) a letter written in 1814 to a Balliol fellow-student in which Lockhart summarizes these attractions :

> " There is a vacancy at present in our Humanity Class.   I was inclined to be very desirous that (Sir William) Hamilton should stand, but he scorned the idea.   For my part I think he was a fool.   I don't well see how they could have refused him on any accounts, although nothing is too base for them ; and I fancy I may count upon your perfect approbation for my sentiments respecting the merits of £1,500 a year—an excellent house, library, etc., and six months of vacation— besides little more than two hours a day of drudging during the session."

There is a similar reference to the privileged life of Glasgow professors in the " Life" of Sir Richard Jebb who was appointed Professor of Greek in 1874 :   " The session is from November 1st. to April 30th, but the work of the last month is comparatively light. Ten days' holidays at Christmas, four days at the end of January, and divers stray holidays, and then the splendid six months."   This arrangement in Arts continued till 1908 or so.

With the growth of the city's population and prosperity the university in 1870 moved to the west end, away from the region of poverty and slums.   The new building has been described as scholarly and intelligent in detail, rather than inspired as a whole. It is dominated by one tall tower supported by a miscellaneous sprinkling of tiny turrets, which distract the vision and defeat the union of dignity and repose.   The site is magnificent.

The college at Aberystwyth was a mere infant in arms when I left it and was still being tenderly nursed by its founders, some of whom I knew in the flesh. Glasgow was hoary with age and only forty years younger than St. Andrews, which reached back five centuries into distant pre-Reformation times. Glasgow owed its university to its Bishop before there was a municipality, and to a Pope, who founded the Vatican Library. In the session 1895-6 when I registered there were nearly 1900 students : 1629 men and 246 women; Arts and Medicine had about 750 each, Science, Law, Theology the rest. Today there are seven thousand. Other differences than numbers struck the student from the south. There was a plentiful supply of bursaries and scholarships—five hundred of them. Class fees were three guineas a class. Many of the students were poor though we all tried to conceal the fact. The Arts classes which met in the forenoon were opened with prayer. A story connected with this is told of Gilbert Murray. Murray when he first came to Glasgow said the Lord's prayer or some other prayer ; then when he became troubled about praying stopped it. A deputation of students came to remonstrate and he compromised by saying the Lord's prayer in Greek.   Then later misgivings returned and he announced that he would not continue to say the prayer and any student who wished to know his reason would be told privately.   Some classes met at eight o'clock in the morning, gowns were scarlet, not black, the Latin class was called the Humanity class, and there was a well-appointed students' union where one could get a hot mid-day meal for ninepence, an easy chair after it and a new book, and thus escape from the stuffy lodging in Clarendon Street, so much more cramped than the two spacious rooms I had enjoyed at Aberystwyth.   Registration cost a guinea and in return you received a card :

Ricardus Robertus Williams,

Civis Universitatis Glasguensis

A Kal. Octobr. MDCCCXCIV ad Kal. Octobr. MDCCCXCV.

The Library took a returnable deposit of one pound, the Union five shillings, a third or fourth hand gown three shillings and threepence. Then there were fifth hand text books and brand new note books. Pennies went on the *British Weekly* and the *New Age*, threepenny bits in the Sunday collection, and many pennies for stamps. There were a score of students' societies which usually charged sixpence or a shilling per session. The premier Society was the Dialectic which met on Friday evenings and claimed, in my time, to be the largest in the United Kingdom. I can illustrate on how little one could live by my weekly bills which for the first six weeks amounted to 11/1d, 9/6d, 10/11d, 10/8d, 10/4d, 10/3d. These included 1/- to 1/3d for laundry. A cooked joint on Sunday, cold mutton daily for the rest of the week and a suppositious fire smothered with coal dust through the winter.

Our landlady, Mrs. Paterson, was an elderly, staid and un-obtrusive widow. She had three sons employed in engineering shops and every morning she was up at 4.40 to see them off to their work. She called Williams and me at 7.30. We slept on a shelf in a cupboard, about seven feet by five, which opened off our living room. This room was rather swamped by an enormous wardrobe used by Mrs. Paterson. Our clothes we kept in our trunks. A what-not held our books, and a rug concealed our washstand when not in use. Experience at Aberystwyth had taught us to limit our conversations with our landladies, as they had a natural tendency to expand and waste time. So of Mrs. Paterson's background and interests we knew nothing. I think the airless cupboard in which

Williams and I slept at night and the meagre meals we shared by day explained the fatigue with which I was always oppressed during my stay in Partick.   We should have asked for more food and somehow paid for it.   After a session, Williams and I left Mrs. Paterson for the University Students' Settlement at Possil Road, and our expenses rose to round about fourteen shillings a week, the increase corresponding to the improvement in our rooms and diet.

The Students' Settlement was established in 1889 under the inspiration of Henry Drummond, four years after Toynbee Hall had been founded by Canon and Mrs. Barnett in Whitechapel. Most of the original settlers were either Free Church folk of evangelical faith or Established Church folk with the kind of religion that inclined them to social service : all but one or two in the first years were, as I was, making for the ministry but there was no thought of restricting membership to any one faculty.   Round about the time I joined the group there was a turning from the ordinary orthodox outlook to a socialistic view of life combined with the Christian. Philosophy was always a predominant interest, especially in its theological applications, but gradually Economics came to take its place. Students from Gilmorehill and from the Free Church College mingled here and took part in club and other forms of social work. The neighbourhood was poor and overcrowded and one would need the hide of a rhinoceros to be indifferent to the misery around us, or to be satisfied with prescribing Moody and Sankey's evangelical salvation as the one and only remedy.   I was allotted a " close " which had forty-four families on six floors on one staircase in forty-four rooms—the famous ticketed houses.   We went about, it was said, unpacking our hopes of a blissful future, with a New Testament in one pocket and a Fabian tract in the other, seeking to reconcile the otherworldliness of the one and the this-worldliness of the other. In 1898 I had a stock lecture on *The Breakdown of Parliament* in which I foretold the early disappearance of the House of Lords and the dawn of the millennium.

In this same year the Queen Margaret Settlement was formed and it led in 1901 to the opening of a Residence in Anderston which ten years later was to become the centre of a School of Social Study and Training in close co-operation with the University. For fifty years the Settlement has been the scene of the untrumpeted devotion of a succession of gifted and unselfish women whose names shine in the hearts and memories of their friends. The one I knew best was Lizzie (or Lily) Lochhead, who left a comfortable lawyer's home in Paisley and a summer house in the Kyles of Bute to work for a life-time in the women's and girls' clubs and camps of the Settlement. She was tiny and trim but tough and quick, could act a part in a play or dance a reel, and her gay spirit and humorous outlook cheered all who met her, while her mastery of the local accent and vocabulary took her straight into the hearts of the surrounding folk.

Universities are conservative bodies and it was less than ten years before my enrolment that Glasgow was brought ' up to date ' by the constitution of a separate faculty of science (1893) and by opening its doors to women for the purpose of study and graduation in the session 1892-93. When one day I fell off a bicycle and bruised my face I called in Dr. Marion Gilchrist, the first woman graduate in Medicine in Glasgow (1894); and on the committee of our Fabian Society I served with Miss Isabella Blacklock, the earliest woman graduate in Arts (1895). There was a women's department of the University at Queen Margaret College and lectures were delivered there, but some Professors refused to duplicate their courses as a waste of time and thus mixed classes in the Arts Faculty became the custom. Men and women students met less easily : there was not, as at Aberystwyth, a covered quadrangle, with a surrounding gallery, over which they could lean or together perambulate. It was

only at this time that chairs of History (1893) and of Political
Economy (1896) were founded.   The preliminary entrance examination had recently been stiffened and made compulsory and to the
dismay of the landladies and the booksellers, the number of
entrants was lower than it had been for fifteen years.

During the nineteenth century, before the New Regulations of
1892, seven subjects were required for graduation and they could be
taken in three groups : Latin and Greek ; Logic, Moral Philosophy
and English Literature : Mathematics and Natural Philosophy.
Commissioners by an Act of 1889 retained seven as the perfect
number for an ordinary degree but henceforward they allowed a
selection from a list of four times seven or twenty-eight subjects
grouped in four compartments.   There are good judges who hold
that for the majority of the students the original compulsory seven
provided a better education than was furnished by the elective
system.   What mainly mattered to me—and it had been one of the
reasons for escaping the coils of the London degree—was that I was
free to get rid of six subjects and then concentrate with the aid of
private tutors on the seventh, mathematics.   This at long last I did
successfully.

A Glasgow Professor of Divinity once classified students as
follows : first came the ' steady' student, who from a sense of duty
works hard ;   next came the brilliant student who wins prizes ;
thirdly (where I belonged) the modest student trying to do his best ;
fourthly, the ' dilettante ' who works by fits and starts ; fifthly, the
' superior ' student, whose efforts, such as they are, are made ' by
way of a special favour to his professor ' ; and, lastly, but rarely, the
' purely frivolous ' student, whose forgetfulness of what he owes to
himself . . . is a less evil than his disturbance of the work of others.[1]

[1] *The Divinity Professors in the University of Glasgow* 1640-1903. By
H.M.B. Reid.

A not dissimilar classification could be made of the thirty-one professors who varied in character, quality, and influence. In the Arts Quadrangle in Glasgow at the turn of the century they belonged to the first two groups, the conscientious and the brilliant. Among the leading lights were G. G. Ramsay (Humanity), William Jack (Mathematics), and Robert Adamson (Logic). It was my fault not to have benefited more from them.

Ramsay for half the year was laird of an estate in Perthshire and for the other half a Glasgow professor, and all the year tall, spare, animated, and something of a martinet. This book is meant for friends in Wales and I cannot resist quoting one passage we were set by Ramsay to translate :

> " I thought I should have found in Scotland a conscientious people, and a barren country ; about Edinburgh it is as fertile for corn as any part of England, but the people generally are so given to the most impudent lying and frequent swearing, as is incredible to be believed.
>
> I rest your Lordship's most humble servant.
>
> Oliver Cromwell."

Ramsay's Humanity class met at nine a.m. and at one p.m. except on Saturdays—" one of the most turbulent democracies in the world ", George Gordon called it. (*The Discipline of Letters*, p. 187.) It was broken up into sections for Latin Prose, a severe and salutary discipline from which one learnt to reflect on the order and meaning of words. You had to rethink the English thoughts in Latin and *vice versa*. It may be possible, with the help of a gradus, to turn out Latin verse with the sketchiest knowledge of the meaning of the phrases used ; it was far less easy to play this trick with Latin prose. Ramsay had a lively if hectoring manner and there was no dodging him if you were not prepared. Your name was shouted rather than called out. You stood up and trembled. " Come along, Sir, don't keep the class waiting." The first line of one of the Odes of Horace runs *Exegi monumentum aere perennius* (" I have erected a monument more enduring than brass"). The student confounding *exegi* with *edi* translated " I have eaten a monument more lasting than brass." " Then, Sir," said the Professor, " you may sit down and digest it." " Why are you unprepared, Jacobus Johnston ?" Ramsay roared to an elderly student, so the story went. And the poor man stammered : " My wife had a baby this morning." Ramsay not hearing him properly retorted : " Don't let it happen again." You read the Latin, scanned the lines, and began to translate.

Student : *Pauper aquae*—scantily supplied with water.

Ramsay : with enormous emphasis : " O dear me, Sir, that will
never do. Horace was a great poet and all great poets are
simple. ' *Pauper aquae*—poor in water ' ".

Student : " *Non ante volgatas per artes* '—' through arts not
previously known.'

Ramsay : " No, no ! ' Previously ' may do for the *North British
Daily Mail*, but not for Horace. ' Not known before '.
Use the simplest Saxon word you can find."

Then, if the end of the hour was near, he would take up the rendering himself and turn the ode into such perfect English that the class would break out into a cheer and he would remark good-naturedly, " I'm sure Horace would feel much obliged." Ramsay had two assistants, a gentle governess, John Brown, who went to New Zealand and was Professor of Classics in the University College, Wellington, for nearly forty years, and the very shy Daniel Rankin, whose sense of duty led him to visit the students in their lodgings in spite of the difficulty he found in making conversation. He was a powerful swimmer but was drowned by being caught in a strong current off the east coast of Scotland.

William Jack, Professor of Mathematics, with his large open
face, light clear eyes, and sandy straggling beard answered to my
notion of a Highland bard. He had at one time been editor of the
Glasgow Herald. He had a friendly genial manner and moved
through mathematical problems with illusory ease. " I wish gentle-
men to take down as many notes as possible and for two reasons.
My notes will be hints not found in the text books, and secondly it
will help to make me speak more slowly." There is a story told of
one of his students doing a geometrical deduction : " Produce the
line AB to L," said the student. " Better keep it within the
University grounds," interrupted Jack. This was one of the classes
not opened with prayer, though Jack's assistant, Daniel Lamont,
was destined to become a Professor of Pastoral Theology and
Moderator of the General Assembly of the Church of Scotland.

Mary Agnes Hamilton has drawn a fine portrait of her father,
Robert Adamson, against the background of his family in *Remem-
bering My Good Friends*. His subject, Logic, did not attract me.
He spoke without a note from an encyclopaedic mind and made no
concessions to the more feeble-minded among his listeners, of whom
I was one. He spoke with such precision that what he gave as
extempore lecture could be printed as delivered. His prestige was
high among the abler students of his subject. The lectures he gave
on the History of Philosophy were published after his death from
the notes taken in class by Hugh R. Buchanan, a distinguished
student. Adamson died in February, 1902, and was cremated at
the Western Necropolis. I remember standing with a group of
mourners at the funeral, watching the arrestingly beautiful face of
his sorrowing wife, while Henry Jones paid a tribute to the worker
at his side, whose life had moved " without break or intermission
along the quiet ways of reflective thought and cast its peaceful light
on the deep problems of the nature of man."

All these and others too I honour in retrospect, but the teachers to whom I owed most were Henry Jones (Moral Philosophy), A. C. Bradley (English Literature), William Smart (Political Economy), and Richard Lodge (History).

Henry Jones had delivered his inaugural address on October 23rd, 1894, to a crowded audience in the Bute Hall with Principal John Caird presiding to the accompaniment of students crowing like cocks, barking like dogs, and shouting *Cymru am byth* (Wales for ever) as the Bedellus, bearing the mace, led the Senatus Academicus to their seats.   I have written elsewhere of my debt to Henry Jones[1] and William Smart.[2]   Their homes were always open to me, their influence was decisive, and I enjoyed their friendship while they lived.   The one made me read much of Plato and Aristotle, Kant

[1] Henry Jones (1852-1922) was the son of a Welsh shoemaker and a servant maid and himself worked at his father's bench before entering Bangor Training College and becoming headmaster of an elementary school in South Wales in 1873.   In 1875 he entered Glasgow University with a Dr. Williams Scholarship worth £40.   His chief teachers there were John Nichol and Edward Caird.   Under Caird, Jones took 1st class honours in philosophy, won " the big Clark " fellowship worth £225 per annum for four years, studied in Germany, and returned to be Caird's assistant.   " Jones," said Caird, " is one of the best men we have had here in my time, with a remarkable combination of Celtic fervour and lecturing power with capacity for philosophy."   He was for a few months in 1883 a lecturer at Aberystwyth where his son was born, later to be celebrated as the author of *The Road to Endor*.   In 1884 he was a candidate for the principalship of the new college at Bangor, but Harry Reichel was appointed and Jones obtained the Chair of Philosophy.   In 1891 he was appointed to the Chair of Logic and Metaphysics at St. Andrews and in 1894 he succeeded Caird at Glasgow.   He had all the gifts of a great teacher— knowledge, ethical passion, natural eloquence, an overflowing gift of humorous illustration, an intimate acquaintance with the Bible and Shakespeare, Scott and Browning.   Dr. James Denney said of him : " He is far the most influential university teacher in Scotland."   He delivered courses of Gifford Lectures in 1920-21 and 1921-22.   They were afterwards published as " A Faith that Enquires."

[2] William Smart (1853-1915) was the first occupant of the Adam Smith Chair of Political Economy in the University of Glasgow to which he was appointed on its foundation in 1896 by Mr. Andrew Stewart, ironmaster.   He had previously spent some thirteen years in the thread business of Clark and

and Hegel ; the other made me realize that there was something to
be said for the capitalist system, though perhaps less in South
Wales than elsewhere. These two Professors, with Bradley and
Lodge, made their students write essays and flattered some of us by
personally criticizing them, leaving others to be dealt with by
assistants. All this work was severely competitive and lists showing our positions were displayed for all to see. An A on the board
was as rare as it was exhilarating. The moment a subject was
announced and the class released there was a wild scamper to the
Library for the " books recommended." I preferred to work in
Baillie's Institution, a small, select, and serious Library in the city,
where in perfect peace and at a furious pace one gutted large tomes,
often a page at a glance, pouncing on what was relevant to the subject in hand and transferring the sentence or paragraph to a note
book for later use. Digestion and compression followed and somehow, in my case always at the last moment, an essay running into
two or three thousand words was handed in, with the ink wet, at
the hour fixed. The knowledge gained by this method was superficial as there was little time for reflection. What we wrote was

Co. of Mile End and Paisley and succeeded his father as a partner in the firm.
During this period he was deeply influenced by John Ruskin and Edward
Caird and took to lecturing on Political Economy first at University College,
Dundee, and then from 1886 to 1896 at Queen Margaret College, Glasgow.
In his next period he was under the sway of the theory of value propounded by
the Austrian economists, Wieser and Böhm-Bawerk, developed on marginal
lines by Professor Alfred Marshall at Cambridge. In 1902 Smart was mainly
responsible for setting up the Glasgow Municipal Housing Commission and in
1905 he was made a member of the famous Poor Law Commission in London,
attended most of its two hundred meetings, signed its Majority Report and
wrote much of its text and many of its memoranda. He was a man of real
ability, little originality, enormous industry and great modesty. He was
always trying to reconcile the conflict between the economic ideal of increasing
productivity and the moral ideal of human happiness and dignity. In
personal relations he was charming and generous, especially to poor students.
His *Economic Annals of the Nineteenth Century* is a work of reference of
permanent value.

derivative and only the presentation could claim to be one's own, but even so the experience proved a useful rehearsal for later attempts to produce memoranda at short notice for political masters. It was my secretarial duty and personal pleasure in 1945 to send, on behalf of the Pilgrim Trust, a cheque for £5,000 towards assisting a scheme for rehousing the Baillie Institution in Blythswood Square.

During the fourth quarter of the 19th century the influence of German idealism, modified by Thomas Hill Green and others, was important and widespread. Most philosophical chairs in England and Scotland were filled by Neo-Hegelians. The Rhine had flowed not only into the Thames but into the Mersey and the Severn, the Clyde and the Firth of Forth and covered the academical world of Great Britain. Looking back to-day I can still recall the exciting experience of advancing for the first time into the Hegelian universe under the guidance of Henry Jones and the books of the Cairds. We will give you the keys of Heaven, they seemed to say, and they opened one door after another : Mind, the ultimate reality, reality the expression of reason ; thought, the unifying of opposites, the partial always passing over into a larger whole where contradiction is reconciled ; art, the triumph of the idea over matter imparting to semblances a higher reality, " born again " through mind ; the individual penetrated and characterised by his relations with his fellows, his soul permeated by, one with, the universal life ; world-history a rational process, an all-embracing unfolding of immanent mind disclosing a growing consciousness of freedom, in progressive stages revealed in ' national minds' or States, all struggling with one another and thereby developing their spiritual powers. Similarly religions evolved through stages from sorcery and phantasy to Judaism, the religion of sublimity ; Hellenism, the religion of beauty ; Rome and the religion of utility and political power.

Finally Christianity which conceived of God as going out of and returning to Himself through self-renunciation and death. He who would save his life must lose it.

The surge and swell of these vast conceptions swept me and others off our feet and it took us some time before we learnt to navigate such deep waters in our coracles.

We became very expert in manipulating Subject, Object and Absolute in our attempts to explain the profundities of religion, philosophy and art, and to resist the attacks of scientific materialism. Subject and object were present within self-consciousness from the beginning. Mind or Spirit was the highest quality which united man to God, the Absolute Mind, the universal completely self-comprehending Subject, where all contradictions were reconciled. The abuse of physical and mechanical metaphors had led to insoluble statements of the problem of character and environment. All the orders of knowledge, all the degrees of reality were distinctions which fell within our finite, human minds. There was no escape from thinking anthropomorphically so long as we were men. Students turned these profundities into platitudes and juggled with all change as progress and the real as rational. As the years passed and I grew to know myself and my fellow-men better, to know my own weakness and sinfulness, my mind returned more and more to the New Testament and, however haltingly, to the Christian faith as more helpful and satisfying an interpretation of the world's mystery than the philosophy of Hegel or the impressive variations of his disciples.

The kinship with Socialism of aspects of Hegelian thought made it more palatable to some of us. The State was a divine idea and a moral agent, but we did not envisage it as totalitarian nor sacrifice the individual to it. Both grew together. " The best State," said Henry Jones, " is that which does most for the

individual and enables him to do most for himself." We knew our
Carlyle but the Hero as Hitler was beyond our ken.   In the Economics class-room we were familiar with the Marxian theory of value
but we had also read Jevons and the works of the Austrian School in
translations : Wieser and Böhm-Bawerk.   On the other hand I do
not recall any close study in the Philosophy class-room of Marx's
transformation of Hegel's teaching into the doctrine of the class war
and the supersession of capitalism by communism.   There is no
mention of Marx in Henry Jones's *Working Faith of a Social Reformer* (1910).   We had not then heard of Kierkegaard (1813-1855)
and his reaction against Hegel.

Bradley's English Literature class met in the late afternoon.
Some two hundred of us listened intently to a spectral figure—bright
eyes, pale face, dark beard—speaking quickly in low tones of the
gravest moral problems in subtle analytical language, balancing and
distinguishing, enjoying and praising with extreme precision and
yet without a trace of pedantry.   The lecturer read without any
oratorical artifice ; he put questions to himself and he answered
them by asking many more on themes uniformly lofty or profound :
Shakespeare's delineation of Iago or Othello, Shelley's treatment of
imagination and love, Keats' vision of the unity of all beauty, the
beauty that is easily come by and is all sweetness and pleasure and
the beauty that is won only through thought and through pain . . . .
His deep feeling when reading some poignant passage acted like a
cleansing fire.   I still remember the thrilling effect when after reading some great lines from Marlowe he added briefly : " Shakespeare
did not die at twenty-nine."[1]   A rare aside, in brackets so to speak,

[1] Compare " We can also observe, upon a little conversance, that the
plays of Christopher Marlowe exhibit a greater maturity of mind and of style
than the plays which Shakespeare wrote at the same age :   it is interesting
to speculate whether, if Marlowe had lived as long as Shakespeare, his
development would have continued at the same pace.   I doubt it :   for we
observe some minds maturing earlier than others and we observe that those
who mature very early do not always develop very far."
                    T. S. Eliot *What is a Classic* P. 11.

brought our teacher nearer to us : " A good many hold a mixed religion. One day they believe that the world is governed by wisdom and goodness, and the next they are afraid of the number thirteen, go to a fortune-teller, or refuse to be married in May." In the *Book of the Jubilee* we saw both sides of him : a *Translation of the Dedication to Faust* and *A Roundel on the Lean Man in Winter* which is short enough for quotation :

> Were I but fat I should not freeze,
> This sooty snow might do its worst ;
> The North might bellow till he burst
> If only I were more obese.

> I should not drivel lines like these ;
> Of poets I should be the first,
>   Were I but fat !

> Wives I should have, and properties
> And morals : all would be reversed :
> I should be blessed who now, accursed,
> Howl to the heavens in agonies,
>   Were I but fat !

At one of his occasional tea parties for a few students I drew him on to talk of Mazzini, of whom there were several protraits on the walls of his flat. I wanted him to write an introduction to the *Everyman* edition of the *Duties of Man*. He promised to consider this, saying that as a young man at Balliol he had been deeply influenced by the Italian and had written an essay on Mazzini's idea of religion which might serve the purpose I had in mind. This plan was not found practicable but there are some pages on the subject in the fourth chapter of his Gifford Lectures, *Ideals of Religion*.

As the session proceeded and we got our essays back, Bradley's fine courtesy in commenting on them humbled us : we felt our standards of judgment rising, our minds being quietly remade. The secret of his power over us lay where Shakespeare's power lay—in the insight which unravels the intricate behaviour of the human mind and heart. This is what absorbed the expositor and commentator and it was this which really most interested his seemingly superficial listeners. He had forsaken the formal study of philosophy only to bring a philosophic mind to search for truth in the realms of poetry. He took the poets seriously and shared and stressed a truth which Bosanquet put this way :

> " The hardest of all lessons in interpretation is to believe that great men mean what they say. We are below their level, and what they actually say seems impossible to us, till we have adulterated it to suit our own imbecility. Especially when they speak of the highest realities, we attach *our* notion of reality to what *they* pronounce to be real. And thus we baffle every attempt to deepen our ideas of the world in which we live. The work of the intelligence is hard ; that of the sensuous fancy is easy ; and so we substitute the latter for the former."[1]

But Bradley had already summed up his life's teaching in his essay on Aristotle's conception of the State in *Hellenica*, in a passage, which I have kept not far from my elbow through the years :

> " With every step in the moralising of politics and the socialising of morals, something of Greek excellence is won back. That goodness is not abstinence but action ; that egoism, to however future a life it postpones its satisfaction, is still nothing but selfishness ; that a man does not belong to himself, but to the State and to mankind ; that to be free is not merely to do what one likes, but to like what one ought ;

[1] Hegel : *Philosophy of Fine Art, Introduction,* xix.

and that blindness to the glory of ' the world ', and irreverence towards its spiritual forces, are the worst of passports to any ' church ' worthy of the name,—every new conviction of such truths is an advance towards filling up the gulf between religion and reality, and restoring, in a higher shape, that unity of life which the Greeks knew."

Richard Lodge, the historian, and brother of Sir Oliver, was not fat but lean and very tall. He had a loud robust voice and, I think, enjoyed lecturing. He was complete master of his subject and had a gift of clear exposition which sometimes rose to eloquence.

> " There was a Professor, R.L.,
> Who never would stop for the bell :
>   When his class showed their ire,
>   He said, ' How can you tire,
> When I lecture so awfully well ?' "

He was a Liberal in politics and was so amazed by Joseph Chamberlain's rectorial address on Patriotism that on the day following its delivery he devoted his lecture to correcting its distortions. " It is not my business in this place to discuss the politics of the Lord Rector, but it is my duty to see that you get your history right," and he hit out right and left in fine style. Alas ! what the Lord Rector's errors were and the Professor's corrections I have forgotten. Chamberlain's opponent had been Birrell, and this is what the Tory students sang :

> Gaudeamus igitur
>   Chamberlain rectore
> Birrell foras jam expulso
> Pringle lacrimis convulso
>   Singulari more.

Vivat semper Chamberlain
Vivat cum honore ;
Pereant hi odiosi
Liberales, ever prosy
With the same old story.

Lodge invited me to read for Honours in History with him, but I was already vowed to Philosophy and Economics. The fogs of Glasgow caused him to migrate to the University of Edinburgh and thirty years later I used to see his aged tall bent figure stooping among the books of the Athenaeum, as if he had a load of them on his back, as he certainly had many of them stored in his capacious memory.

Looking back I realise how little I knew of the famous teachers in the departments of Science and Medicine. I knew personally the refined physician, Ralph Stockman, Professor of Materia Medica (1897-1936), whose studies of rheumatism and arthritis are, I am told, of continuing importance. He cured my wife of an acute attack of muscular rheumatism by deep massage, using a masseuse trained in his own method. This was the painful dispersal of fibrous thickenings by deep knuckle rubbing day after day for four or five weeks, followed by a course of soothing peat baths at Strathpeffer. Sir William MacEwen arrested attention by his strikingly tall and erect figure and his rapidly spreading reputation as a pioneer in brain surgery.

The Union Debating Hall was arranged like that of the House of Commons. Women predominated in the galleries. Members of the Government turned up in evening dress. Irish members came armed with flutes and bagpipes. The Division was taken at 10.20 p.m. It was much harder to raise a cheer or a laugh from this audience than from the benches at Aberystwyth. The subjects debated were the perennials : " That the French Revolution was

Photo by] [Annan & Sons, Glasgow

THE UNIVERSITY OF GLASGOW

conducive to the welfare of Society", " That Strikes are justifiable", " That the growth of democracy means the decay of romance." Robert Horne, F. A. Macquisten, Hugh P. Macmillan, John Buchan, and George Adams belonged to a slightly earlier generation than mine ; Buchan was already a legend as the precocious author of *Sir Quixote of the Moors* and *John Burnet of Barns*. Of Horne, Macmillan, Buchan and Adams I was to see much in a future then hidden : Horne, brought up in a manse in a mining district, as a clear-headed and ambitious Cabinet Minister, a nonchalant Minister of Labour and teller of stories innumerable, Macmillan and Buchan as Pilgrim Trustees. With all his splendid gifts John Buchan when backing an opposed appeal for a grant could not parry his tougher fellow-Scots, across the table—Macmillan and James Irvine, who quickly overpowered him with a stroke or two. Adams went to Balliol with a Snell Exhibition. I was to recommend him to Lloyd George in December 1916 for a place on his personal secretariat, where he was of great value in dealing with Irish questions as a liaison with Horace Plunkett, chairman of the Irish Convention. W. M. R. Pringle became famous as an expert heckler of Ministers in Parliament. Brailsford, to-day an outstanding journalist and welcome broadcaster, was Adamson's assistant before he went to fight for Greeks against Turks ; he has kept out of Parliament, but has spent much of his life criticising it. He was a leading member of the University Fabian Society when Ronald Burrows was its President, Norman Leys its Treasurer and I its Secretary. Sidney Webb and Ramsay MacDonald came from London to speak to us. MacDonald had the appearance and gifts of an orator ; Webb emitted a series of uniformly-shaped sentences, one after another, delivered in level tones and all addressed to the understanding. MacDonald with a natural Highland eloquence spoke of the divorce of the pulpit from the people and control of

28 WELSH BROTH

the Press by the capitalists : democratic articles meant a shrinking income from advertisements : working men could not become members of parliament because of the expense involved : the I.L.P. was the legitimate heir of the progressive party and in the evolution of politics it could not have been born earlier than 1893.

Burrows was an assistant to Gilbert Murray and a keen Anglican. I called on him, having heard of his progressive views, and suggested the formation of a University branch of the Fabian Society. He responded with enthusiasm.

Judging by a letter addressed to me from the General Secretary of the Fabian Society, Edward Pease, dated February 1897, which has survived, I must have been a fairly active provincial member. Here are two paragraphs from it :

> " We are fully alive to your suggestion as to the need for books. We have under discussion two proposals for meeting this : first, to print some of our tracts, e.g. in particular, " Labour in the Longest Reign," now in the Press, in book form, and, secondly, to issue a Fabian series of books by distinguished Fabians. The latter proposal, which has been under discussion for five years or more, has now reached a form which promises well. Your approval of the project will carry weight.

> " I note what you say as to lectures which agrees with our experience here. I think your proposal for studies of politics of divers countries a most admirable one. The methods of the German Social Democratic party are so simple and obvious and, up to a certain point, so effective, that their universal applicability is much too readily assumed. Mr. Reeves was expounding to me two days ago the failure of that particular method in New South Wales and South

Australia, where (at any rate in the former country) an independent party obtained a larger proportion of followers than anywhere else. Your scheme has the merits of novelty and I think is admirable."

Gilbert Murray, like John Stuart Mill, a saint of rationalism, was not a joined member of the Fabian Church, but an Associate and nearer the Kingdom of God than many of us in the front pews. For the space of twelve hours Murray was a member of the Society. On the night of Sidney Webb's address he signed the Fabian Declaration, but recalled it in the morning. Our theory was that his wife, Lady Mary Murray, a good Liberal, brought him back to the straight path. It was whispered that she was a thorough-going egalitarian and took tea with the maids by turns in the kitchen and in the drawing-room—and almost certainly in leadless-glaze teacups. The poisoning of workers in the china and earthenware industries in Staffordshire had roused public sympathy and when I married Eirene Lloyd in 1902 we took some trouble to obtain leadless-glaze china for our first home at Balmore, Torrance of Campsie. From the Chief Inspector of Factories I obtained a list of Glasgow shops providing the best conditions for their workpeople. We joined the local co-operative society and I remember going with James Morton, of Sundour Fabrics fame, on a deputation of two to the manager of the Scottish Co-operative Wholesale Society at Shieldhall to try and induce him to employ better designers of household furniture for working-class use and enjoyment. But he could see nothing amiss with the current designs and we made no impression.

* * * * * *

I remember the furtive beginnings of the Labour Movement in South Wales. Capitalism was hardly challenged in the seventies as a social philosophy, but Trade Unions were fighting successfully for legal recognition. Co-operation was a separate social ideal but feebly represented in the coal valleys. The first meeting of the Rhymney Socialist Society was held, not in a hall, but in the cricket field; some sixty or seventy young colliers were present and strung themselves on the grass along the boundary hedge in the twilight. In March, 1899, my mother was writing to me :

> " Its the election on the brain here now. Willie [my
> brother] says they are going to put three socialists in. Willie
> is fully employed with committees, unions, lit. and deb. etc.
> Willie Wright [Fabian lecturer] is here very often now. Mass
> meetings, lectures. I am glad that people are beginning to
> open their eyes. I think the tide is turning for the best. Poor
> people shall have better houses, better pay, everything."

The first meeting of the " Socialist Bodies of the West of England and the South of Wales " was held on November 7th, 1896, in a coffee tavern in Caerphilly, with about twenty men and one woman present. Richard Roberts, afterwards the Rev. Richard Roberts, D.D. of Toronto, was in the Chair. The woman was later to become known as Mrs. F. H. Spencer, D.Sc. She was then Amy Harrison who taught at Bridgend County School,[1] lived at a Settlement while studying at the London School of Economics, became a research secretary to the Webbs, and joint author with Miss B. L. Hutchins of the *History of the Factory Acts*. She and Dr. Roberts were students and contemporaries of mine at Aberystwyth.

Keir Hardie had founded the Scottish Labour Party in Glasgow in 1888, and the Independent Labour Party followed at Bradford in 1893. I had joined the Partick branch of the Independent Labour Party within a few weeks of arriving in Glasgow ; my membership card is dated 13 December, 1895, and I am credited

---

[1] See Beatrice Webb, *Our Partnership*. P. 153.

with having paid fivepence in that month. Keir Hardie was President, Tom Mann, Secretary, John Lister, Treasurer. Throughout my years there I was in touch with other branches and other forms of the Labour Movement in the days of its despised infancy, when if it did not meet in holes and caves of the earth, it managed to find their urban equivalents in obscure halls. I first met Robert Smillie in November 1896 at a meeting of the Christian Socialist League in Glasgow. He had the same text then as when I met him in Downing Street thirty years later—the hardships of the miners. He made words burn and sting. Every year one in three of the miners employed were either killed or injured; they earned seventeen shillings per week, while the Fife Coal Company was paying dividends of from twenty to thirty per cent. We were not bound by a narrow economic doctrine ; our approach was ethical or rather we were striving to bring the economic and religious factors into a right relation. Our propaganda took the form of lectures to small literary and debating societies in church and co-operative halls ; public meetings for well-known speakers from London ; the founding of the socialist weekly *Forward*, by Tom Johnston, who edited it for twenty-seven years, and survived to become the most widely admired Secretary of State that Scotland has ever had. It was a thrilling time of splendid hopes, this birth and youth of the Labour Movement. Poverty need not be, ugliness need not be, wars need not be, so we thought and taught. We wanted a classless society but not a class war.

      " Socialism is the reign of human love in room of hate. Socialism means that the land of Wales will again belong to its people . . . and the pits and railways and docks and ironworks and steelworks and tin works should all belong to the people and not to the few only. If this were the case . . the ugliness and squalor which meet you at every turn in some of

the most beautiful valleys in the world would disappear, the
rivers would run pure and clear as they did of yore, and woods
would again cover the mountain sides in which many birds
would make sweet melody, while in spring the lambkins
would sport on the lea and in the summer the full-uddered
kine would come home lowing in the gloaming."

So ran Keir Hardie's address to the electors of Merthyr in 1900,
and it was plain that he drew his inspiration from the Bible and
Burns, from Ruskin and William Morris, rather than from Marx and
Engels.   He read *Sartor Resartus* at 17 in an attic by the light of his
collier's lamp three times in succession and the spirit of it and of
Past and Present entered into him.   Henry George's *Progress and
Poverty* followed later.   Hardie had the texture of a poet and the
resonant voice and speech of a prophet.   At a soiree, to raise funds
for the branch, he would shed his importance and delight the
comrades by singing *Annie Laurie*.   He exchanged the tweed cap
and plaid muffler in which he made his way from West Ham to
Westminster for a broad-brimmed sombrero and this with the large
head, bushy hair and beard, flowing tie and Scottish accent all combined to captivate the fervid Welsh miners and from 1900 Hardie
championed their cause in Parliament.   Merthyr had need of him :
it had the highest death-rate of the seventy-six large towns in the
quarterly table issued by the Government.

For years Hardie travelled to meetings innumerable, large and
small, night after night, speaking for a pittance, and in the *Labour
Leader* week after week for years he wrote his heart out.   The
Sermon on the Mount had often been his text.   The outbreak of
the War saw the ruin of his hopes and he was probably not unwilling
to depart this life when he died in September 1915.

On the evening in July 1945 when the amazing Labour victory
was announced, it was natural that Mr. Attlee's first words to the

comrades assembled to greet him were: "If only Keir Hardie were here to-night."

We were the light-bringers, music-makers, dreamers of dreams, movers and shakers, prophesying to the old with Messianic fervour the message of a new world coming, but we did not then imagine it would take fifty-three years before we should see Labour in power and still longer for the arrival of the empire of justice and brother-hood. Only slowly did I learn, with William Morris, " how men fight and lose the battle, and the thing that they fought for comes about in spite of their defeat, and when it comes turns out not to be what they meant, and other men have to fight for what they meant under another name."

It is customary to speak of Socialism as producing one dead level of society and contrasting this with the infinite variety which results from unmitigated competition. I pictured the drastic modification of the latter but the complete attainment of the former, a literal equality, was not only inconceivable but undesirable. Compromise is of the essence of any British Utopia. To raise the squalid level of the poorest, to elicit their starved energies and aspirations, to reduce the oppressive power of the few at the summit, to advance by some degree the solution of the chronic conflict between quality and quantity, this was what in our coolest moments we envisaged, hoped for, worked for.

We were not the only reformers in the field. There were the Vegetarians and the Anti-Vaccinators, and more influential still were the disciples of Henry George whose panacea was the Single Tax. Some sought salvation in living together in communist or co-operative colonies on the model of Owenite experiments. They were usually pacifists, hostile to a centralized state and to a machine civilisation. I have the prospectus of one of these before me based on the colony at Ralahine, County Clare, and applied by a group on

a farm near Newcastle-on-Tyne, in 1896. "This Association," it
ran "being constituted on the principles of Liberty and Equality,
we do not recognise any other authority but the one of Reason,
and no member or members shall have any power but that of
Reasoning. A Joint Committee shall meet every night to dis-
tribute work. All fundamental points to be discussed until unanimity is established. No working time shall be fixed or limited,
as we believe that . . . each one will do his best."

I believe these experiments always failed in this country, but
in the large and lonely spaces of the frontier States of America some
flourished for many years so long as they kept themselves from the
pollution of the profit motive or the *prima donna* fever. The
Perfectionists of Oneida and the Inspirationists of Amana were
examples. Their secret was the religious sentiment which bound
them together ; when it weakened dissolution was not far off. The
same is true of the Labour or Brotherhood Churches which sprang
up at this time. One hears little of such attempts to-day because
their lesson has largely been learned.

In this Glasgow period I married and my wife and I shared in
the women's struggle for the vote.[1] In Labour meetings I had met
Enid Stacy, Caroline Martyn and Mary Macarthur, young women
who gave themselves to the uttermost to the Cause and whose
influence I feel still persists among those who knew them. I now
met Lady Frances Balfour, Mrs. Pethick Lawrence, Ethel Snowden,
and Mrs. Bruce Glasier—all remarkable speakers. Mrs. Pankhurst
stayed with us when it was "not the thing." In 1942 I met Lady
Snowden again when she visited me at Harlech and presented the
Library of the College with some six hundred volumes of English and
French Literature, the great poets and the great novelists, most of

[1] See p. 60.

them in mint condition. A bust of her courageous husband—a replica of the one in the Treasury in Whitehall—adorns the Library.

In the election of 1905 I worked for George Barnes against Bonar Law in the Blackfriars Division of Glasgow. After his victory by some 300 votes, Barnes and his wife rested with us for a few days at our home, now in East Kilbride. He was the salt of the earth and I felt he retained his savour to the end. He came down to breakfast " in his braces " i.e. without vest or coat, and with shirt sleeves tucked up. He was too solid and stiff for the acrobatics of party warfare and by the time I met him again as a Cabinet Minister in Whitehall Gardens he had long ceased to count as an effective leader of Labour. Lloyd-George found Barnes helpful, and took him to Paris. His last years were devoted to furthering the League of Nations. He was the only Cabinet Minister I saw using a dictaphone.

After one of the meetings in the east end of Glasgow in support of Barnes at which I presided and Cunninghame Graham spoke, " Comrade " Graham took me to George Square, where stand the municipal buildings. He wanted to see the Square by moonlight. Across Kelvin Park and a short walk from Gilmorehill was Kelvingrove Art Gallery and one of its most attractive exhibits was Sir John Lavery's handsome full-length portrait of " the uncrowned King of Scots" as Graham was sometimes called.

* * * * * *

My political activities at this time were not confined to Glasgow. In South Wales I spoke with Tom Mann in halls and in the open air, two different operations. He was then in the early forties, a powerful figure and an overwhelmingly eloquent speaker. As a youth in Birmingham he had been familiar with the oratory of Bright and Joseph Chamberlain, had come under the influence of the temperance movement and seriously considered taking Anglican orders. But he was too restless and individualistic a Socialist to stay long in one organisation. When I knew him he was Secretary of the I.L.P. and then active in founding the Workers' Union. After a day full of " demonstrations " and endless talk and when the last comrade had left our lodgings, he would take off his coat, and write far into the night, covering sheet after sheet. I never knew whether he was writing articles for the Cause or letters to a wife or a sweetheart. On one occasion we arrived at the station at (I think) Bedlinog where we were met by the local branch of the I.L.P. with a brass band and a procession lined up behind ; the band struck up a martial air, the horses plunged forward but the carriage did not move. Some youngsters had secretly detached us, and the Movement was momentarily halted and humiliated. Soon after I heard Tom Mann had turned publican, and was tenant of *The Enterprise* in Long Acre. This did not last. He went off to Australia, got put in prison, and came back in 1910 to preach Syndicalism.

In the spring of 1904 at the invitation of their leader, Tom Richards, I spoke to the miners at their annual demonstration at Bargoed in the Rhymney Valley. My theme was the social aspects of Trade Unionism—really a plea for the establishment of what we would to-day call Community Centres, needed to fill the vacuum between the chapel and the public house. From the mass meeting the executive adjourned to a local inn for an enormous feast. To reach the dining-room upstairs I passed through the bar and this left on me the lasting impression that sometimes a great picture in chiaroscuro does. The room was crowded not with men from my audience, but with colliers coming off from some shift, homeward bound, in their working clothes, covered with a mixture of coal dust and grease, as were their streaked and grimy faces. They were all gulping down beer and the room was so full that I had to rub against them as I pressed my way through ; the air reeked of stale

beer and was thick with the odour of the coal-pit. I experienced
an instantaneous and unforgettable physical revulsion, utterly un-
worthy of a Christian or a Comrade. My last words on the plat-
form outside had been :

> " Millions of money will be paid away in wages here in the
> next ten years, but will homes be brighter, manners sweeter,
> children merrier, ten years hence ? These are the questions
> that matter. These are the questions I leave with you."

All through the gross meal upstairs I was haunted with what
I had just seen and with my distance from, not my identity with,
these men. The contrast between the serious and sober and
thoughtful demeanour of the audience I had just been addressing
and these slaves of appetite was not to be explained or justified by
the pressure of poverty, of the capitalist system, of chapel-going
hypocrisy. Indignation with " the system" was blunted by the
fact that the sheep and the goats dwelt as neighbours in the one
community. If religion was the opium of the one, alcohol was the
opium of the other. I knew then that there were other uncontrolled
appetites just as anti-social if less openly and disgustingly brutish.
Perhaps I was, even in 1904, conscious of what the Labour Movement has suffered from the loss of gifted leaders who " clog their
minds with beer and whisky "[1] I certainly have been conscious of
it since.

It was only slowly as I discovered and faced weaknesses in
myself that I learnt to make allowances for those of mankind. I too
was a sensualist in thought if not in act. I too knew the sadness of
failure, the bitterness of remorse, and learnt to be tolerant, com-
passionate. " Every life contains black spots of shame," confessed
Bishop Hensley Henson. Where all are sinners or victims it would,

---

[1] *Beatrice Webb.* By Margaret Cole. P. 75.

as Chekhov said, " be strange not to forgive." In Bargoed I was probably revolting against the unmitigated ugliness of the scene. I have seldom found drunkards, on or off the stage, amusing or picturesque.

Why did I not stand for Parliament ? I was sounded, quite seriously, by more than one Welsh constitutency. Members were then unpaid—that was an obstacle which might somehow have been surmounted. I had no overweening ambition for public life and then and always have preferred anonymity to advertisement. This may have been more cowardice than shyness. I saw two sides of a question and thought the policy of helping any party travelling the gradual Fabian way worthy of support. I knew too much of the causes of poverty to imagine that it would be easy to abolish them. Religion, education, legislation all would be needed.

On May Day, 1909, I spoke with Philip Snowden at the Pavilion, Caernarvon, to the quarrymen, and urged them to develop the educational side of the Union by asking the College at Bangor for a tutor. This was done and the first class was started in 1910-1911 at Blaenau Ffestiniog, in charge of J. F. (later Sir Frederick) Rees. What I chiefly remember of this meeting was the masterly way in which D. R. Daniel, once secretary of the Union, made the Welsh language talk economics when moving a vote of thanks. I had found doing this so difficult when preparing my speech that I turned to Robert Richards, M.P., for help. Since then the language has made great strides and can now talk Jung and Freud. Daniel belonged to the class described by the early Russian novelists as ' superfluous men ', by French novelists as ' cut out of cloth which has no thickness ' of whom we have examples in Wales—brilliant talkers, full of good impulses, devoid of will-power, content to puff

[1] The first Tutorial Class was held at Wrexham in 1908-9 under the Oxford Joint Committee with R. H. Tawney as tutor.

rings of smoke from *cigarettes enchantées*. With them to do a thing
and to say they had done it was the same. They were poets of
sorts. In his charming futility, Daniel was in complete contrast to
the energetic friends of his youth, Tom Ellis and David Lloyd-
George, whose early lives he recorded.

* * * * * * *

To return to Glasgow. Long before Keir Hardie in Ayrshire,
there had been another rebel in New Lanark, Robert Owen, and
there had also been in Glasgow itself a social reformer and illustrious
churchman, Thomas Chalmers, who was not a rebel by temperament,
but a believer in rank and subordination. Owen was the less
commonplace, the more original figure, and his doctrine was closer
to the course of nineteenth century practice. Chalmers attempted
to deal with the poverty of his parish on a church basis and by en-
listing the co-operation of the poor themselves. He achieved remarkable results through the power of his personality, his administrative energy, his superb oratory. Had there been in Scotland as
many Chalmerses as parishes—though he denied this—the social
problem might have shrunk to negligible size.

The coming of the Poor Law in the 'thirties placed the responsibility for the poor in official hands and made voluntary support
supplementary. Parishes were grouped into unions and the unions
made responsible for providing funds and administering them. But
even in the Scottish Act of 1845 the imposition of a parish rate was
not obligatory and the duty of administering relief was entrusted to
the Kirk Session, the heritors and magistrates. In England the
problem centred round the relief of the able-bodied : in Scotland,
the able-bodied were not relieved by the Poor Law. Broadly
English Poor Law administration was characterised by profusion,
Scottish by parsimony. The problem in Scotland was to secure

adequate relief to all persons legally entitled to it. It was essentially a system of outdoor relief and it was repugnant to Chalmers as undermining thrift and independence. He reigned in Glasgow from 1815 to 1823. In the fifty years which followed, the city tried thoroughly neither his prescription nor those of the rival physicians.

But the Glasgow of my day was regarded as having carried municipal socialism further than any other city in the kingdom ; the water supply was municipalised in 1855, gas in 1869, rehousing in 1871. And not only in respect of gas, water, housing, electricity and tramways. The Town Council was experimenting with insurance, pensions, model lodging houses, free concerts and a minimum wage of a guinea a week for Corporation workmen. They had also obtained an Act of Parliament enabling the Corporation to buy insanitary property at the valuation of the ground on which it stood. These measures were not at first regarded or denounced as embodiments of theoretical socialism so much as manifestations of common sense in the realm of local government. Socialist propaganda began in the eighties. Doctrinal opposition on party lines was to come later but it was not until 1933 that the Corporation had a Labour majority. The big rehousing schemes were still in the future. In the nineties sinks and a water supply had been put in and the plan of building a brick shaft against the back wall of the tenement with access from the staircase allowed for one water closet on each floor serving, three, four or more families. This was regarded as a notable advance. But the Medical Officer of Health, Dr. J. B. Russell, could still report in 1888, that 30 families of each one hundred lived in houses of one room, that 70 per cent of the city's population occupied houses of one or two apartments. " When Scotland brought from France the tenement house, she omitted to bring the concierge." Ticketed houses (with a metal ticket stating the air space and legal number of adults permitted), City Improvement

Trusts, Housing Commissions had all been tried, and had made some but no radical impression on the problem.

The Glasgow Workmen's Dwellings Company with Sir John Mann as Secretary, experimented usefully in the nineties by erecting new blocks and renovating old ones, chiefly of one and two-roomed houses, and *placing them under the management of a resident caretaker.* This was their special contribution based on the example of Octavia Hill. Rents were roughly two and three shillings per week and tenants were selected from those whose household earnings were under 20s., and under 25 shillings per week. Between two and three thousand persons were accommodated in this way. Dividends never exceeded 4 per cent. Other pioneers of this reform working through the Kyrle Society were Mrs. Ada Reith, mother of Lord Reith, and Miss Marion Blackie, a member of the family of publishers. Years later (1923) I urged Bonar Law, then Prime Minister, to tackle the Glasgow problem in some more drastic way. He sent his secretary (now Lord Davidson) and me to see Lord Weir, and Weir produced a scheme for the standardized manufacture by a central Corporation of 100,000 houses, to let at from 5/- to 8/- per week, to be made of concrete or steel. But the opposition of the building contractors, on the one hand, and of the trade unions on the other, defeated this praiseworthy enterprise. In the 'forties, Lord Weir again attacked the problem on a larger scale, and meeting with rather less obstruction, a considerable degree of success has been achieved.

The Lord Provosts around 1900, James Bell, John Ure Primrose, Samuel Chisholm, and especially Daniel Macaulay Stevenson were of a quality which would have worthily adorned ministerial posts in Whitehall, as John Wheatley did later. Stevenson was a constructive pioneer as well as a rich donor, with some of a donor's idiosyncracies. I once deliberately and of malice aforethought, introduced him to Lionel Curtis, who promptly proceeded to relieve him of £40,000 for the British Institute of International Affairs at Chatham House.   This is a sort of usefulness I have found congenial throughout my life and not a few rich folk are indebted to me for skilful surgical operations on their dropsical bank accounts.   Afterwards Stevenson could not thank me enough for providing him with this opportunity of promoting international understanding.   The electrification of Glasgow's tramways, the foundation of its free libraries, its financial system and musical culture owed much to him. He more than any person helped Mann to raise a capital of £40,000 for the Workmen's Dwellings Co. He was one of the University's large benefactors.   For the idea of the Citizenship Trust—a Lectureship in Citizenship—he was indebted to Henry Jones.   They were good friends, but obstinate fighters, and they wrangled long over the tenure of a professorship, the donor wishing it to be in periods of five years, and not as customary *ad vitam aut culpam*. Five years is still taken as the normal length of tenure of the Lectureship.

* * * * * * *

Political Liberalism had done a fine work in opening all problems in heaven and earth to discussion, in removing entrenched privilege, in enabling the common man to count as one at the ballot box, but when confronted with economic inequality and chronic distress Liberalism offered no radical prescription.   In the first decade of the century many of us were harassed with the unemployment which cursed the great cities and were engaged in breaking up the problem into comprehensible parts.   A useful distinction was made between cyclical unemployment and chronic under-employment. The popular term 'unemployed' covered all sorts of gradations of skill and character from the corner-men, short service men, to the specialised craftsmen thrown out by a change of trade process.

Many were low-skilled casual labourers, and half of those who were helped by distress committees in Glasgow, Edinburgh, Dundee and Aberdeen were under forty years of age—in Glasgow over sixty per cent. This fact pointed to the futility of filling labour colonies and relief works with adult inefficients while we manufactured a fresh supply out of news boys, errand boys, van boys and uneducative, unprogressive labour in factories. And some of us did what we could to call public attention to the need for the sort of training which in years to come was to be prescribed in the Fisher and the Butler Acts for boys and girls of fourteen and upwards. In 1906 over 700 boys were engaged in street trading in Glasgow, and in the same year over 1400 between the ages of 14 and 21 were charged with theft and other offences.

Casual dock labour along the Clyde was an allied problem on which I spent some time as University Lecturer, interviewing stevedores, foremen, and lodging-house keepers. The quays were the receptacle for the residuum of failures, moral and economic, from above. They took the flotsam and jetsam from all classes and gave back nothing in return. It was a difficult community to organise ; its essence was its low-skilled quality and casual habits. In Liverpool, the philanthropic Booths and Rathbones had achieved some improvement. There the minimum period of employment was half a day and wages were paid weekly. They had more inward cargoes than outward. In Glasgow the reverse was the case and wages were paid at the end of a day or a job and men could give or be given an hour's notice to quit. Two samples showed an average weekly employment in Glasgow of 2½ days per man, compared with 3 days in Liverpool. Big money, earned by abnormal spurts, was misleading. I examined the books of a Glasgow stevedore working for several companies. An individual trimmer might earn 15s. by a day and a night's engagement (10 hours at 7d. an hour, 11 hours at

1od.). But taking 77 working days there had been work on 35, and if the total money earned had been equally distributed over the men employed, the average weekly wage would have been 6/6d. The varieties of conditions in the two ports made broad comparisons unreliable. And, of course, one found snobbery at these social levels. A general cargo man would consider himself affronted if asked to handle coal. The Trade Unions fought mainly to raise the minimum engagement ; they resisted the limitation of employment to a minority of individuals. They argued that this would create the complete unemployment of the surplus and the practice would be extended to the building trades with a like result. The lack of system suited the employers who could count on more men offering than they needed and also on the Poor Law, charity and debt to help to keep the supply in being when work was scarce.

The inherent weakness of trade unionism was quite clear in the 'nineties : it was a negotiating and a fighting force, but it could not give us socialism. Along with the progress of the unions had come a dangerous sectionalising spirit. The skilled worker did not behold his brother in the unskilled. And machinery was more and more placing the skilled man outside the protected area. Many then saw the defeat of private capitalism in the spread of municipal trading, others thought a time would come when the unemployed would out-number the employed and that they would announce Labour's Armageddon.

* * * * * * *

No one could live in the neighbourhood of Gilmorehill or indeed at the Settlement without being made aware of the influence of organized religion. Everywhere there were churches with graceful spires or massive pediments and pillars. It was something of a shock to reflect that the same city could exhibit the church parade of Great Western Road on Sunday morning and the Hogarthian orgies of Argyle Street on Saturday night. Glasgow without whisky was as inconceivable as Glasgow without sermons. And it may be true that the fierce creative exertion of vast industrial communities, night and day, cannot be sustained without the accompaniment of brutish alcoholic satisfaction. In recent years the cinema has made for sobriety, but in 1900, Glasgow was the most drink-sodden city in the Kingdom, if I may record an impression I cannot prove to be correct.

If the Church had not continued the social teaching and practice of Chalmers after his death, it had led opinion in other fields of Christian endeavour, especially in promoting biblical scholarship at home and missionary work abroad. In my time, there was at the Free Church College in Glasgow, a group of teachers of the calibre of T. M. Lindsay, A. B. Bruce, James Denney, and George Adam Smith. Of these, the last was the most active in social work. He was President of the Scottish Council for Women's Trades, of which Margaret Irwin was the indefatigable secretary. It produced numerous reports on sweating, overcrowding, juvenile labour, and did what it could to quicken the civic conscience about these evils. Bruce in Glasgow, and Marcus Dods in Edinburgh, were applying scientific methods to the study of the Bible, and mediating the change over into the modern conceptions of its composition. Dods in his inaugural address to his students had quoted with approval the grand sentences of Milton :

> " They are the troublers, they are the dividers of unity,
> who neglect, and permit not others, to unite those dissevered
> pieces which are yet wanting to the body of truth. To be
> still searching what we know not by what we know, still
> closing truth to truth as we find it (for all her body is homo-
> geneal and proportional), this is the golden rule in theology
> as well as in arithmetic, and makes up the best harmony in a

church, not the forced and outward union of cold, and neutral
and inwardly divided minds."

The bald Calvinism of the Westminster Confession, he urged, was
partial and one-sided, and a theology truly Catholic must serve
itself heir not only to Calvin and Augustine, but also to Clement,
Origen, and Athanasius. Not the least advantage of residence at
the Settlement was the mingling of divinity students with the rest
of us and they helped to keep us abreast of the freshest theological
thought. It was, for example, well to compare what Henry Jones
was preaching at Gilmorehill with what James Denney was teaching
at the Free Church College. Denney was at once a Puritan and 'a
blade of Damascus.' His intellectual power and evangelical fervour
had great influence on generations of students. He pleaded hard in
his Church for a simplification and shortening of the creeds ; in the
war of 1914-1918 he crusaded for drastic public control of the drink
trade. To strangers, he was apt to seem brusque and curt and
terribly in earnest, but those who, for example, read his article in
the *Glasgow Herald* on *Burns and Present Distress* (January, 1917),
knew there was in him deep understanding of human frailty. " We
must reluctantly admit," he wrote, " that our national poet has
provided us with a far less wholesome creed (about drinking) than
Shakespeare has made authoritative for our neighbours." "Whiles,"
confessed Burns, " but aye owerlate, I think braw sober lessons."

On Sundays, many students made their way to Trinity Church,
to hear Dr. John Hunter preach to a congregation which not seldom
filled the aisles and pressed on to the pulpit stairs. Hunter was a
native of Aberdeen, and came from Hull to Glasgow in 1886 when
he was 37 and, with a brief interval, remained there till 1913. He
was a close friend of P. T. Forsyth and had been attracted from
Calvinistic theology by F. D. Maurice. Hunter read with passionate earnestness and at great speed, a sermon of sublimated

gospel. And not only the sermon but the hymns and prayers were purged of the crude realism familiar to more evangelical congregations.

One of the ablest men at the Settlement was the Warden William Boyd, who was to become Reader in Education at the University and author *inter alia* of *The History of Western Education*, familiar to students. We were recently to rekindle our friendship of 1900 when in 1949 he visited Aberystwyth as an Examiner in Education. The most outstanding character amongst us was a medical student, whose work for the natives of Kenya was later to attract attention and arouse controversy, Norman Leys. His contemporary and mine, John Lyle Morison, in a tribute to Leys on his death, in August 1944, told how the British Government had committed itself to two contradictory policies : the proclamation of trusteeship on behalf of the tribes and the concession to British settlers of the best portion of the land. Leys protested against the planting of the tribesmen on the poorer lands and was defeated. His basic view was that far more weight should be given to African wishes and a large and real share of power be given to educated African minorities. Leys, as Morison adds, had in him the stuff of which Livingstones and Gordons are made. I disappointed him because I could not make Prime Ministers read his books or squarely face the problem of Kenya. He forgave me a little when the Irish Treaty was signed, but I always felt I was made of inferior metal to him. He was religious, unafraid of authority and most unwilling to compromise with wrong-doing. His devotion and tenderness to patients were inexhaustible. His combative down-rightness did not make for promotion or even employment and he paid a heavy price in health, in pocket, and in peace for his deep and rare sincerity. In reply to a letter of mine he wrote on 31 August, 1918 :

" Thank you very much indeed. I had an astonishingly

warm letter from His Grace of Canterbury. He went even
further than I should go in saying that policy in Eastern
Africa would soon become a burning question in national and
international life. I am just beginning to write in spare
moments a memorandum on the subject, how to put into
action the wise policy for tropical Africa. Hawkins's tract
on internationalism was disheartening. It matters nothing
what constitutional arrangements are made about *Sovereignty*
so long as actual control remains in the hands of the triple
alliance of capitalists and absentee estate holders, politicians
like Capt. ——, and public servants like your acquaintance ——.

" I shall know in a week or two whether I am forbidden to
return to Africa on health grounds. I hate to think my
hopes may be finally destroyed. But I shall be thankful to
leave a service where I have been treated like a traitor and a
scoundrel. I am afraid I make a very bad martyr. In the
bottom of my soul I crave for a little personal prosperity
while I know perfectly well that it is ruination to my usefulness to let personal interests enter my mind at all. If I am
finally invalided, Kenneth wants me to apply for a job at
home on the strength of fourteen years public service. But
I fear I am a bad bureaucrat, and I fancy I ought to prefer a
quiet country practice.

" I know you must be unhappy about the Prussianising of
our government and country. I wish you would go but I
realise that things look differently from the inside. But I
don't feel sure the inside view is the truest. The Russian
adventure is the final proof to me that the actual control of
the Government is in bad hands. I believe you can serve
your country best as a Labour M.P."

Kenneth (1876-1950) was Norman's younger brother. Dr. Tawney has written of him in the *Oxford Magazine* (9 Nov. 1950). Kenneth was apprenticed to a firm of Chartered Accountants, a profession for which he was not obviously fitted. He completed his apprenticeship and I encouraged his desire to leave it for academic life and so did Professor Smart. He began an Arts Course at Gilmorehill in 1898 and went to Merton College, Oxford with an exhibition. After a short period on the staff of the History department at Glasgow he returned to Oxford and settled down for thirty years with a tutorial fellowship at University College, and spent the last eight years of his life as Vicar of Isel, near Cockermouth. He had an acute analytical mind and severe standards of scholarship which inhibited publication. In the background he helped his brother with his books on Kenya. Otherwise he lavished his gifts on generations of students.

At one time we shared a room, and on a certain evening I was finishing an essay on Carlyle for a university prize. It was due to be put in Principal Story's letter-box before midnight. Leys was reading Acton's Cambridge inaugural on history, and rolling out sentences nearly a page long. He challenged me to quote the longest in my essay. I did this with sufficient skill to mask its irrelevance and to win the prize.

Among our friends was a broad-chested, spectacled and intelligent assistant in the College Library who had a fine reading voice and not once or twice did we persuade Irving Morgan to read aloud to us some essay, play or poem without interruption from start to finish. The spell turned on the single performer and uniform voice. I can now recall only three of these pieces : Vernon Lee's *Ariadne in Mantua*, Max Beerbohm's *The Happy Hypocrite*, and Mrs. Hamilton King's *Sermon in the Hospital*.

* * * * * *

At the end of the session 1897-98 I spent a Sunday at Seacombe on my way to Rhymney and my host remarked that I looked tired : " We'll go on 'Change tomorrow and see if we can find you a berth on a tramp steamer." The result of this diaconal intervention was one of the best holidays of my life. I have since voyaged in the *Berengaria* and the *Mauretania*, dressed for dinner in both and hardly known I had left Claridge's. A tramp steamer is different and I prescribe it to students who can command five shillings a day for a month or two and a couple of pounds for laundry and tips. On May 12, I signed on as purser in Barry Dock, and left laden with coal for Genoa in the *Isle of Anglesey*, known among sailors as one of the Ham and Eggs boats, because of the bountiful treatment of their crews by the old-fashioned North Wales Calvinistic Methodist owners, in contrast with some pagans, domiciled in Cardiff, who would skin a flea for its hide.

In the nineties trade was brisk between the ports of the Bristol Channel and those of Spain, Italy and the Black Sea. It was carried on by steamers of which the *Isle of Anglesey* was typical, doing about two hundred miles a day. They took coal or patent fuel out and returned with oranges, currants, wheat, or iron ore. We had a cargo of 1800 tons and 250 tons of bunkers. Ten years old, the *Isle of Anglesey* had made eighteen voyages to Barcelona and only two beyond, of which this was the second. The captain was forty and had spent twenty-eight years at sea and knew less of his native Aberystwyth than I did. The first mate, from the same town, had been thirty years at sea, had been shipwrecked four times, and though he weighed nearly twenty stone he had never sunk to the bottom. The chief engineer was English from Cardiff, the second, Welsh, from Bethesda, and the son of a quarry manager. The total crew was about twenty-two ; of these, the firemen were the most troublesome ; they were apt to malinger and two deserted the ship during the voyage.

The captain was of diminutive stature, wore uniform and stood on ceremony only when in dock or on shore. His favourite attitude on the bridge at sea was to stand with cap well back on his head, binoculars in his left hand, a pipe in the corner of his mouth and his legs astride forming an equilateral triangle with the deck, one trouser end turned up several inches, the other full length falling over his woollen slippers, and usually neither collar nor tie. He swore only for emphasis, unlike the crew in the fo'csle, whose vocabulary was so limited that they constantly had recourse to swear words to express their few ideas. The captain beguiled his spare time weaving a mat of many colours for his wife at home and mingling ' penillion ' of a tap-room flavour with famous Welsh funeral hymns, gliding from one to the other as smoothly as his ship through a calm sea.

I had been allowed to bring a companion for the voyage, Lewis Miles of Aberdare, who had an all-devouring appetite. He shared the engineers' mess where nothing came amiss : tinned lobster or mackerel, cheese and onions, jam, cucumber and currant cake, all travelled together into the stoke-hole and became fuel and power. I, on the other hand, was squeamish, had to be carried to the chart-room amid-ships on deck and was daily and frequently sick on nothing at all for the two months we were away. I was sorely tempted to desert with the firemen. But my endurance was rewarded. For years afterwards I hardly knew the meaning of fatigue.

With my hero-worship of Mazzini, Genoa was of all the ports of the world the one I should have chosen to visit. On our first evening there the Captain and the Chief Engineer took me to see the palaces of the Marble City. This meant calling at a series of wine-shops in the main streets. I knew it was not safe to drink water anywhere on the Continent, except perhaps in Switzerland, where Calvinism had exercised a strong sanitary influence. I avoided spirits and took a little wine at each house of call, but enough to bring me unexpectedly to that blissful condition for which the Welsh have a phrase : *Glan meddwdod mwyn*, ' the sweet verge of drunkenness.' I remained quite clear-headed and able to contemplate my legs objectively, but I had some difficulty in planting one foot in front of the other firmly on the pavement, each leg was inflated and as uncontrollable as a balloon. Looking back nearly fifty years I am able vividly to recall the pleasant exhilaration of this unique experience.

Next day, alone, I found Mazzini's birthplace in the Via Lomellina, and his austere grave in the Campo Santo marked by two upright plain stones supporting a transverse slab with the two words GUISEPPE MAZZINI, all in sharp contrast to the surrounding rows and rows of realistic and sentimental white marble figures. For a few lira I hired an interpreter and went to the university. In the entrance court were three tablets to the memory of Mameli, the two Ruffini brothers, and Mazzini. Will you kindly translate? said I, taking out my notebook and pointing to the Mazzini tablet. The guide stuck in his elbows, opened and spread out his palms in the will-you-buy-a-watch style, and then jumbled out " Very great man, very fine man, lover of his country, Liberty, Equality, Fraternity, you understand, dzhentlmen ? We go now," he went on, quickly changing the subject, " to the bronzes by Giovanni of Bologna." But I was not to be put off. Some students had gathered around us and one of them hailed a professor as he went up the staircase and brought him back. " No, he had no English ; would Latin do ?" " Certe, certe !" I jerked out as though I had been a medallist in the Glasgow Humanity Class, and, pretending to understand more than I did, I gathered a fair notion of the three epitaphs.

We left Genoa light and made for Chanak on the Black Sea

there to await orders.   A few miles out I tried shovelling overboard the ashes from the boilers we had not been allowed to discharge in the port.   Some ship's officer had prescribed this exercise as a cure for my malady, but I steamed with sweat and I blistered my hands in vain.   Painting the ship red, white, grey, and chocolate likewise brought no relief.   I decided to leave all manual labour to Miles and settled myself on the bridge reading Meredith's and Thackeray's novels through the long sunny days under the flawless blue sky of a Mediterranean June.   When we reached the Isles of Greece I put down Thackeray and took up, not Byron, but the *Acts of the Apostles* and read it through, duly reporting the meritorious act in my letter home.   There was no wireless in the 'nineties and our hunger for news could be satisfied only in port, or perhaps when we picked up a pilot a little way out.   I could not learn the result of the school board election at Rhymney until I found the *Merthyr Express* awaiting me at Constantinople.   But much the most important news to reach us—at Genoa—had been of the death of Mr. Gladstone, and at Constantinople I bought English papers with accounts of his funeral.

We lingered at Chanak sipping Turkish coffee from little toy cups.   I chatted with the Greek pilot from Ithaca and told him how Brailsford had gone from Glasgow to fight for Greece with the Foreign Legion, and how I had signed the petition calling upon Lord Salisbury to stand by the Armenians and Cretans.   We talked of Mr. Gladstone : " No man like him after him again," sighed the Greek.

We were ordered to Taganrog in the Sea of Azov.   We stayed a few hours in Constantinople, but the customs officers and shipping agents fussed and bothered and made sight-seeing impossible.   A year earlier ten or twelve thousand Armenians had been massacred in the streets, and there was still a feeling of semi-panic ; for hours we were cooped in the ship chandler's, up a narrow staircase, in a narrow street, and the glories of St. Sophia were denied to us, going and returning.　We had to anchor twenty-six miles out of Taganrog, with a score of other ships.　We loaded wheat brought alongside in lighters from the Don.　A chain of labourers carried the grain in baskets on their backs and tipped them into the buckets swung by a crane into the hold.　They were ill-clad, bare-footed, wild-looking men, who worked from daylight to dark, living on rye bread, dried fish, and weak tea.　At meal times they squatted in circles tailor-fashion around a communal bowl of tea, into which they dipped their tin cups, eating lumps of sugar separately, and munching huge chunks of bread.　There were fifteen of them and they were paid for loading 2000 tons in from four to five days, £3 6s. 8d. apiece.　Some were thieves ; others just feckless.　One was a broken-down clerk who told me proudly that he had seen Salvini in Othello.　I remembered Andrew Bradley telling me the same thing.　The clerk knew a lot about Stepniak, but nothing about Prince Kropotkin.　He summed up his life to me : Ship — work — money — shore — brandy — no money — ship — work — — the Russian version of the Glasgow dock casual.　When the job was done, the ship was washed clean and thoroughly disinfected with some strong tar which I can still smell.

We left Taganrog for Malta, again to await orders.　This meant prolonging our voyage indefinitely.　Miles and I decided to make for home by transferring in Valetta to the *Craigmore* bound for Rotterdam with a cargo of planks.　This took all our money.　I had been told that raisins were a sustaining diet.　In Rotterdam we lived for a day on raisins and crossed on the night boat to Harwich, reaching London on July 7th, fit and hungry and with fourpence. There was a strike raging in South Wales, so a penny went on the *Daily Chronicle* ; a penny each to a bootblack, and a penny to reserve.　Being Thursday, we made for the City Temple, not only to hear Joseph Parker preach, but to find some Welsh minister who would be likely to give us a square meal. At once we spied Richard Roberts, whom I have mentioned earlier, and after the service, he fed us at the Holborn Restaurant. Miles was worried about the next step. I had not told him that I had written from Malta and arranged that our railway fares to Aberdare and Rhymney should be waiting us at the office of the Fabian Society, deposited there by Amy Harrison.

I never had such a perfect holiday again, until I stayed with the Flexners at their camp in Northern Ontario, but I helped others later to have similar cheap facilities, sometimes with the help of the late Lord Essendon of the Furness Withy Line. One such proved fruitful. Albert Mansbridge, his wife and their son went a voyage on a tramp ship from Swansea in 1910. "As on starry nights in the Mediterranean we talked with the crew it became clear to us that something ought to be done to help men on ships in reading and study."[1] Out of this experience and Mansbridge's creative mind was born the Seamen's Library, the Seafarers' Education Service and the College of the Sea, which in years to come were to be helped by the Pilgrim Trust. " You never can tell."

In 1900, at long last, I completed the seven subjects required for a pass M.A., was given a scroll autographed by Principal Story and thirty professors, won a (Bertrand) Russell Studentship at the London School of Economics (£100), a Clark Scholarship at Glasgow (£50) and was appointed an Examiner in Economics at St. Andrews. Many years later I was able to thank Sir Kenneth Clark for what his grandfather had done for me, and I am glad to think that through the generosity of the anonymous founder of the York Trust and the wise co-operation of its secretary, Mrs. Sibyl Jerome, I have been

---

[1] Mansbridge *The Trodden Road*. P. 106.

able as its chairman to dispense many thousands of pounds to help poor students struggling for higher education and professional training.

The Russell Studentship brought me to 10, Adelphi Terrace (in the upper rooms of which lived the newly-wedded Bernard Shaws), to sit at the feet of Edwin Cannan, Goldsworthy Lowes Dickinson and Graham Wallas. W. A. S. Hewins was the Principal, and in his lectures he drew on the German economists, Schmoller and Wagner, making vast generalisations on the course of European economic history. Cannan, on the other hand, was concrete and his lectures were the concentrated argument of a clear-headed Englishman with both feet on the ground.

At the School I had two private pupils, each at five shillings an hour. Miss T., the daughter of an Australian member of parliament, was an earnest seeker after economic truth, and she planned to enlighten her countrymen, and help them in shaping their raw emerging civilisation on the eve of Federation. It was then a community of four millions, supporting fourteen Houses of Parliament, a Governor-General and six State Governors. She found few women to share her progressive views on her return and was too finely bred to face alone the rough and tumble of colonial politics— as we then described them. But conditions of life did not press and depress as in the old country. There was breathing space, elbow room, clear skies and warmth. There had been, it was true, seven years of drought, and the sweetest Christmas carol of all had been the falling of the golden rain-drops in December, and now the marvellous recuperative powers of the land would soon make it flow again with milk and honey. So she wrote to me in 1903 after two years at home.

The other pupil, an Austrian Count, was the product not of a raw but of an exhausted civilisation. He had known comfort and

refinement on a small estate in the neighbourhood of Vienna, and
was a Socialist of the parlour.   I found him to be more interested in
ethics than in economics and over luncheon in a Jermyn Street
restaurant he wanted me to justify the ways of God to man.   He
had the half-humorous, half-cynical weariness of a man who has
tasted many pleasures and found them unappetising.   He had tried
the usual prescriptions for happiness open to a man of wealth.   I
added to the list the obvious duty of looking after his workpeople,
housing and paying them properly, caring for the health and education of their children.   He wrote me a grateful note before he returned to Austria and shortly after I heard that he had committed
suicide, not, I hope, as the result of trying my prescription.

Through some of the winter sessions at Glasgow, I lectured at
the Athenaeum, a sort of polytechnic, to bank clerks, would-be
accountants and others, among whom I picked out a plumber and a
tea-taster and made life-long friends of both.   Generations of
students are usually forgotten because they were never really
known.   They may remember you.   Once or twice I have been
startled at being recognized in a London theatre, between the acts,
by some victim of my Gilmorehill lectures.   Of my two Athenaeum
friends, one was a Socialist and the other a Liberal.   The one,
William Tweeddale, became the most reputable master-plumber in
the West of Scotland, and the other, James Paterson, a Provost of
Milngavie.   Paterson grew into the good citizen who provides
" utility goods," the backbone of local administration in church and
state.   He brought integrity and independence to the service of the
Mechanics Institute, the Penny Savings Bank, the Nursing Association, the Red Cross Society, the Sessions of the United Free Church,
and the Bowling Club.   When the World War came, he was put on
government committees and asked to advise on the distribution of
tea in Scotland.

Tweeddale's patronymic had been Twaddle. The transformation to the colourful and aristocratic version took place as a condition of marriage to a Lecturer in History at Gilmorehill to whom he proposed at Nyeri in Africa. The engagement was a by-product of a meeting in the Dark Continent of the British Association for the Advancement of Knowledge, and the marriage which followed in due course was a great success.

The family plumbing buiness had started in the neighbourhood of Glasgow Cross, in 1848, when each plumber had a boy attached to him throughout the seven years' apprenticeship, had to carry a fire with him and a pot of solder with a ladle wherewith to fashion the contraptions needed. Fifty years later the business was in the charge of two brothers, William and James, and their sister (now Mrs. George Lindsay). The one brother was eager and expansive, the other quiet and practical. In 1905, William visited America and returned stored with new ideas which he proceeded to apply to a succession of big housing and factory contracts. The plumber who tinkered with taps and cisterns was becoming a sanitary and heating engineer. The firm was called upon not only to install indoor bathing pools in the mansions of an opulent minority, but to strip the roof off the cathedral, and to run up the lightning conductor of the Tolbooth steeple. He was a pioneer in Scotland in equipping large blocks of flats with central heating and hot water. Alongside this ever-growing employment as sanitary engineer in Scotland and London, with contracts embracing hotels, cinemas, banks, hospitals and houses, went the most varied public activities of an athletic altruist. William Tweeddale was Scottish Amateur Champion Rower in 1900, and responsible for the two big boat houses on the Clyde by Glasgow Green. He was President of the Scottish Unitarian Association, a leading advocate of the Sunday opening of the Kelvingrove Art Galleries, chairman for over twenty years of the

Glasgow Fabian Society, a President of the Economic Section of the
Royal Philosophic Society, an active worker on the committees of
the Scottish Council of Women's Trades, and Queen Margaret
Settlement. All this irrepressible and unselfish energy went with
a character of rare modesty and gentleness. He and his wife are
commemorated at the University by annual prizes awarded in the
departments of Political Economy and History.

In April, 1901, I took a First in the Honours School of Economics and Philosophy, thanks to the Principal allowing me to sit
the week's examination in the forenoons and evenings. I then, and
since, have preferred to sleep in the afternoons—indeed, like
Hannibal, Napoleon, Cobden, Lloyd-George and Winston Churchill,
I can fall asleep at will at most hours of the day.

Taking exercise I have usually found to be a dreary occupation.
Two or three times in Glasgow I went with the philosopher, Norman
Kemp Smith, to a Gymnastic Class, but I was soon bored with
inhaling and exhaling and chose a couch instead. Some enterprising Butlin or Lyons should provide in big cities silent padded
parlours where tired sightseers or somnolent civil servants could
hire a berth and recreate themselves with half an hour's sleep, without the necessity of taking a Turkish Bath. Not everybody can
belong to the Athenaeum Club.

I was always indifferent to popular sports and a failure at golf,
though I paid the club subscription for a few seasons. I could not
keep my eye on the ball, and was no better when I was told in a
printed guide that my failure to make a good stroke was due to the
misdirection of the habitual use of the mechanisms throughout the
organism. I had not in fact " the will-to-do " and could not be
bothered to put the " means-whereby " principle into practice.
Golf can become a serious affliction. I once coughed at Criccieth
when Lloyd George, then Prime Minister, was addressing, not the

multitude, but a small white ball, and I only narrowly escaped having my head sliced.

* * * * * * *

An offer which reached me in March, 1899, had made me decide to remain in Scotland. It was from Professor Smart offering me fifty pounds if I would assist him in the following session in reading examination papers and essays, and in lecturing to the Political Economy class, if permitted by the Court. Later he raised this to £250, and told me not to rush off and get married at this sudden and vast accession of income. But knowing better, that is what I did, in December, 1901, to Eirene Theodora Lloyd, who had gone from Aberystwyth via a teaching interval at Blaenau Ffestiniog, with a Goldsmith scholarship to Newnham College, Cambridge, and on to the Sorbonne. No £250 invested by a Professor of Economics in an Assistant ever brought a richer dividend of happiness.

This love affair was at first not approved by my sisters, for it was a breach of the promise never to marry which I had quixotically, if honestly, made to them. My celibacy was conceived not only as part of an ascetic ideal but also as making it easier for me to repay them for their support during my long stay at college. Fortunately, Eirene Lloyd, far from taking me from them, returned me to them, strengthened to help them, and my sisters quickly found in her a precious friend and a warm welcome in our new home.

We were "quietly" married in the vestry of the United Methodist Chapel in Grove Street, Liverpool, by two friendly Presbyterian ministers, R.R. and the Rev. Richard Jones, Llandinam, who had agreed to use the Service which we had, with uncompromising integrity, written for them. If asked at that time to what church we belonged we said we were Greek Christians or Christian Greeks, thus acknowledging our debt to the two strands of our faith, "the reconciliation of Galilee and Parnassus." As I remember this defiance of orthodox convention, it was a medley of noble thoughts on love and duty interwoven from the Bible and the writings of Mazzini and Ruskin.

After "the wedding breakfast" the bride and bridegroom caught a tramcar and then a train to Glasgow. Many years were to pass before I felt at ease in hailing a taxi. Similarly I fought as do some Labour Cabinet Ministers against wearing evening dress, but finally conformed to custom. My Professor taught me much besides Economics and I gradually found *de minimis* a principle of wide extension. I was but a Young Man from the Provinces slowly discovering myself in an irrational Society.

We had found a cottage at Balmore, Torrance of Campsie, ordered a bed, a table and chairs to be made for us by Arthur Simpson of Kendal, a Donegal carpet from the 'Sundour' Mortons, and for the rest draped a few Tate's sugar boxes with Liberty curtains. We had the courage of our income and could wait. Young couples who furnished their houses of a morning or an afternoon in Sauchiehall Street missed the detailed and extended enjoyment which was ours to distil drop by drop when seeking what we wanted from the craftsman who made it. Charles Macintosh, an original architect (associated with George Walton, who built what is now Coleg Harlech) had newly startled Glasgow with his School of Art and Kate Cranston's Tea Rooms. His geometrical patterns anticipated the moderns but he had more influence abroad than at home. In the spirit of *l'art nouveau* he and his hardly less gifted wife, designed everything for a room, including, I remember, anaemic knives and forks for table use, and spoons with flattened bowls, fitted to carry a delicate ration of soup. My wife and I became furniture-conscious. Whenever possible we visited the workshops and discussed the wood, the fabric, the shape, the colour of the chair or carpet, the fender or footstool, the tray or the basket, buying one or two things at a time according as the rise or fall of the barometer at the bank allowed. It was a red-letter day when we proudly unpacked a carved oak side-board from Kendal. Simpson is the carver mentioned in Gordon Bottomley's poem *Littleholme* :

> " A carver at his bench in a high gable
>   Hears the sharp stream close under, far below,
>   Tinkle and chatter, and no other sound
>   Arises there to him to change his thoughts
>   Of the changed silent town and the dead hands
>   That made it and maintained it, and the need
>   For handiwork and happy work and work
>   To use and ease the mind if such sweet towns
>   Are to be built again or live again."

There is a morality of things as of persons and we never regretted having these examples of honest worksmanhip about the house. In years to come this collaboration led us to know examples of the best domestic work and the makers of much of it : Peter Waals, who had been Ernest Gimson's foreman : the younger Barnsleys ; Charles Voysey and his wallpapers ; Harold and Phoebe Stabler and their enamels and silverware and pottery ; Alfred Powell and his plates ; Louise Powell, scribe and illuminator ; F. L. Griggs and Fred Richards and their etchings ; Alex Miller, woodcarver. I never knew Edward Johnston, but I possessed his epoch-making book *Writing and Illuminating and Lettering* (1906). It was one of a series of technical handbooks edited by W. R. Lethaby, whom I met with Sidney Greenslade, the architect of the National Library of Wales and of our own little house in Thanet. Of Lethaby, Eric Gill said that he was one of the few men of the 19th century whose minds were enlightened directly by the Holy Spirit. There was, about several of these craftsmen, a saintly quality. My acquaintance with some of them I owed to Molly Bernhard Smith of the Twenty-One Gallery. This was in the Adelphi within easy reach of Whitehall Gardens. In later life on my way back to the Cabinet Office after lunch, I often dropped into the tiny gallery which did much to launch young and unknown artists. One of Epstein's early exhibitions was held here in 1913, soon after the trouble over his Wilde monument in Paris and the statues in the Strand. The "Polynesian monstrosities" in the little room in the Adelphi aroused the ire of most critics, but the sculptor was championed by a no less original poet, T. E. Hulme, in the *New Age* on Christmas Day, 1913. Here also a little later the works of other Futurists were shown : Edward Wadsworth, Frank Dobson, and the sculptures of the Serbian Mestrovic. When the Gallery moved to Mill Street, off Conduit Street, it was out of my way, but I remember shows of lithographs by Spenser Pryse and the drawings of Robert Austin and Graham Sutherland. All these young men owed much to M.B.S., who introduced them to American, as well as to English collectors. It was through Joseph Thorp, 'Mr. T. of Punch,' I met a maker of beautiful books, St. John Hornby, and at Shelley House, on the Thames Embankment, was allowed to handle his Ashendene treasures. I enjoy the possession of books bound not only by George Fisher at Gregynog, but by the younger craftsmen, Loyd Haberley, Sydney Cockerell, and Roger Powell. Lunching one day at Whitehall Court with G.B.S. and Charlotte Shaw, the question of binding a special edition of his collected works came up and I suggested the use of a cloth coloured jade green in honour of Ireland. A few weeks later we met again and I brought with me to lunch James Morton of Sundour Fabrics, with his little bag of samples of cloth, and the Shaws had invited Emery Walker to meet him. Jade green was agreed upon and on Shaw's 74th birthday I received an inscribed set of the thirty-three splendid volumes which now repose in the Elphin Library at Coleg Harlech.

What choice spirits these men were, what beautiful things they fashioned or sponsored ! " maintaining the fabric of the world, and in the handiwork of their craft was their prayer." It is on this side of their education that our students are starved : they are rarely over-come by the sheer beauty of any work of man which their eyes behold.

But I must return from this digression. I had just got married (December, 1902) and presented my wife with the latest and fattest edition of Mrs. Beeton's Cookery Book, one of the few subjects she had not studied and which she soon mistressed, and we found a young woman near-by who could clean and shine and also type my lectures. I recall these early months, the prelude of thirty-five years of happy companionship, as alternately supremely blissful and wretchedly miserable, while we sought to adjust our tempers to the task of living together. " Zadig found by experience, that the first month of marriage, as it is written in the book of Zend, is the moon of honey, and that the second is the moon of wormwood." It is hard at thirty-one to bid farewell to fixed habits, and to do what should be done when it ought to be done, whether you like it or not. I am still learning this lesson. It was impossible in the new home to forget the old. I was the eldest of nine children ; two died in early childhood and seven grew up to adult life. I now brought three brothers to Balmore and found posts for them with Glasgow firms. I meant well but the direct transplantation to the great Scottish city from the small Welsh village was not entirely successful. Of my three sisters, the eldest married and died in Rhymney in 1934 ; to the other two who looked after the original home to its end, my debt is heavy.

* * * * * * *

In June, 1901, the University of Glasgow, founded in 1451, celebrated its ninth jubilee, and scholars from the ends of the earth gathered to do it honour and to be honoured in turn. They came from Calcutta, from Cracow, from California. At the commemoration service in the Cathedral the preacher unfolded the pages of history from the day on which Pope Nicholas the Fifth sanctioned the founding of a university in this remote northerly region and conferred on it all the privileges of the university of Bologna. This was some forty years before the discovery of America in 1492 and not long after the first printed book had made its appearance. It was in 1494 that Aldus in Venice began his typographical career at the sign of the anchor and the twisted dolphin, symbols of stability and speed. Oliver Lodge brought homage from the youngest British university, Birmingham : " As you felt to Bologna," he said, " four hundred and forty-nine years ago, we feel to you to-day." The Vice-Chancellor, the venerable Principal Story, presided over the congregation of divines and doctors in their splendid orange, scarlet, ermine and sable robes. And there were famous women present : Emily Davies and Constance Jones from Girton, Mary Bateson from Newnham, Emily Penrose from Somerville, and Agnes Weston, the Sailors' Friend.

It was the duty of the stewards, gowned and equipped with white wands, to lead the celebrities to the dais where addresses were presented and the capping took place. While the organ played *Men of Harlech* I led the Welsh delegation from Aberystwyth : the President, Sir John Williams, M.D., the Principal, T. F. Roberts, and the Professor of Greek, J. W. Marshall. Williams and Marshall were old Glasgow students. The ceremony over I took them, without notice, to my flat where my mother improvised a luncheon. We could only make the crockery and cutlery go round by washing them between the two courses. The talk was on the hoary controversy of Science v. Classics, Sir John championing Science and Welsh, and the Principal holding out for Greek and Latin as best for Welsh boys. On the next day I led up for honorary doctorates : Sir Ian Hamilton, Principal Alfred Hopkinson of Manchester, and Professor Hubrecht of Utrecht. I chatted with the Marquess of Dufferin, then seventy-six, Lord Lister representing the Royal Society, Sir Henry Roscoe, and the genial Henry Jackson of Cambridge, who told me that his real reason for accepting the invitation to Glasgow was that he might see the crypt of the Cathedral, having as a boy read Scott's account of it in *Rob Roy*. Kelvin delivered an oration on James Watt and Smart on Adam Smith, but neither could be well heard in the Bute Hall. There was also an oration on William Hunter who had provided the university with a museum and had Gibbon and Adam Smith among those who listened to his lectures.

I met Sir John Williams again in December, 1913, at the Lion Hotel, Aberystwyth, when he had just become President of the University College in succession to Lord Rendel. He was already the first President of the National Library of which he was the principal founder. He had just passed his 73rd birthday and I found him, with his pleasant soft voice, full of reminiscences of his early career. He left the Normal School, Swansea, when seventeen, for the University of Glasgow where he spent the session 1857-58. He had not then worked out any plans for a future career but he took Mathematics under Professor Blackburn and lodged in Stanhope Street. John Caird was minister at the Park Church and Dr. Raleigh at Elgin. The ministers who mainly influenced Williams in his early manhood, he told me, were Richard Glover, David Charles Davies and Henry Pulsford. His two chief medical teachers were Sir William Jenner and Sydney Ringer, at University College Hospital, London. After serving as House Physician, without pay, at U.C.H., at Brompton Hospital and at the Children's Hospital,

Great Ormond Street, he returned to Swansea as a general practitioner for three years. In this period he repaid his mother money he had borrowed from her and he saved £1000. Then Providence took a hand.

Dr. Tom Griffiths put up at Swansea for a weekend Dr. Frederick Roberts, Manchester, who was returning from performing an operation in Pembrokeshire. Williams learnt from them that there was a vacancy for an Assistant Obstetric Physician in U.C.H., and that he could get it. He went to London and found he was too late in applying. He saw the Dean. The post was readvertised and he got it. Here again there was no pay, but in ten years he was making about £1000 per annum, and in fourteen years about £4000. Princess Beatrice of Battenberg was expecting a baby in December, and Queen Victoria wanted a physician not too old. Sir William Jenner had two names before him and selected John Williams. Then followed a rapid growth of his practice. He retired at 63 and leased a house at Llanstephan but it looked east and was enervating, so he followed his Library to Aberystwyth. Two or three other things he told me. He had been at University College when Principal Thomas Charles Edwards was a student there, but he never heard him preach. He was often summoned professionally to Scotland and the South of France but rarely to Wales. When a member of the Welsh Church Commission, over which Judge Vaughan Williams presided, Sir John moved a vote of censure on the chairman and (Principal) J. H. Davies seconded. The motion was put by Sir John and carried by five votes to three. The Judge wanted one report.

I next saw Sir John in 1919 again at Aberystwyth when he presided over the College Council and I was one of the rejected candidates for the principalship, as I shall relate in its proper place.

For the sake of the uninstructed reader I ought to add that this eminent physician who attended at the births of numerous royal personages and was the recipient of many royal honours, devoted a great part of his eighty-six years to exchanging his fees for books and manuscripts with the express object of founding the National Library of Wales. For a score of years it was known that he was prepared to buy Welsh books or books concerning Wales, and in this pursuit he was aided not only by famous booksellers like Quaritch, but by a band of expert and enthusiastic laymen who deserve honourable mention : John Gwenogvryn Evans, John Humphreys Davies, Henry Owen and J. Deffett Francis, himself the founder of the art gallery and art library at Swansea. The result of the co-operative labours of Sir John and his friends was a foundational gift of 1200 manuscripts, over 25,000 printed books, together with several thousand maps and plans, drawings, prints, photographs, picture postcards, "and every other form of graphic delineations of matters concerning Wales and the Border Counties." *Si monumentum quaeris circumspice.*

The year 1901 was also the year of an International Exhibition in Kelvingrove Park. What remains with me is the memory of the bang and blare of a succession of regimental bands whose music induced and sustained a gaiety of mood in the sombre community throughout the months of a fine summer. I recall too, perambulating the grounds with that ' flame of the spirit,' Patrick Geddes, watching the coruscations of his genius weave themselves, like the fireworks around us, into enchanting patterns, as he stroked his beard and ejaculated appeals for approval in a caressing voice. He was a wandering scholar who moved through centuries, civilizations, religions with fantastic ease, affixing polysyllabic labels of his own coining to each or to groups of them in a way which at the moment was as impressive as it was incomprehensible. You suspected that no one could talk so much and talk sense all the time. After his death his widow (Lilian Brown of Paisley, an old pupil of mine), invited me to Montpellier to advise her about the future of an international college which Geddes had founded there, mainly with her money. It was impossible to get from her any data for a profit and loss account. She had the sweetest disposition but a mind as untidy in matters financial as her husband, and she could organise neither him nor the college. So his attempt to marry the cultures of East and West on the shores of the Mediterranean perished. He died in 1932 and though few today remember the professor at large who originated regional surveys and town-planning, his seminal ideas are sprouting in the books of Lewis Mumford and others.

Geddes was only one of many visionary projectors I have met. Ebenezer Howard, shorthand-writer, came to Glasgow to tell us of his dream of Garden Cities. Another idealist was sanguine he could make Glasgow a smokeless city and sought help to experiment with extracting oil from coal when that attempt was more novel than it now is. I introduced him to Lord Davies and Sir James Morton as I knew they had more money to burn than the inventor. Years later a popular novelist came to me with a plan for moving the unemployed from Durham and South Wales to Peace River in Western Canada, under the auspices of the Prince of Wales. I went some little way with this and as some millions of money were necessary a Cabinet Minister sounded " The City" and was referred to a bold projector called Hatry—this was fortunately just before he crashed. Objections from the Canadian side would in any event have blocked the scheme.

* * * * * * *

In 1905 Professor Smart was made a member of the Poor Law Commission, and I was attached as one of the Special Investigators.

This meant much travelling between Glasgow and London in
sleepers and long spells in London and elsewhere in the holidays.
Lunching one day at Toynbee Hall I met R. H. Tawney, newly
down from Balliol and then acting as secretary to the Children's
Country Holiday Fund. I divined his exceptional quality at once
and easily persuaded Smart to add him to our over-taxed staff.
Tawney had not been long in Glasgow when Dr. Wallace, editor of the
Glasgow Herald, asked Smart if he could provide a leader-writer
competent to deal with the Tariff Reform campaign. " The paper
is going Free Trade and there's nobody here who knows enough
about it." Daily, in leader after leader, Tawney pursued and
demolished the Protectionists with his pungent pen and scathing
prose. His field of operations widened and on one Monday morning
in March, 1907, there appeared a leader on the smashing defeat on
Saturday of the Progressives by the Moderates in the London County
Council election. It was written on Sunday night when the editor
was away and concluded thus :

> " Well, Londoners have made their choice and they must
> abide by it. They have decided they will be moderately
> housed, moderately educated, moderately clean. It would
> not be surprising if the result of this election should prove in
> the long run to have given, not a set-back, but an impulse,
> to municipal activity, because it will cause men to meditate
> on first principles. When the toad is under the harrow it
> may begin to learn wisdom."

This was too much for one of the directors who protested from his
country seat in Ayrshire. Dr. Wallace was tenderness itself. He
offered to be a father to Tawney and to guide his pen with a blue-
pencil, but Tawney had already had one father and did not want
another. So presently he transferred to the *Morning Post*, then
under (Sir) Fabian Ware, and wrote leaders in place of (Sir) William

Beveridge, whom Lloyd-George had summoned to Whitehall to deal with unemployment.

I had myself started reviewing books on Economics and the Social Services for the *Herald* in 1899. When the Poor Law Commission Report for Scotland came out I filled a whole page of the paper, eight columns, with a summary of it (November 2nd, 1909), which produced a satisfactory feeling in me and a substantial cheque. I had only once before reaped a similar satisfaction, without the cheque, when the *Ulster Gazette* printed a verbatim report of a Barrington lecture, which filled six columns. I still dream of filling a page of *The Times*, and not a mere turn-over, and but for the scarcity of paper in recent times would once have done so.

The rôle of investigator for the Royal Commission on the Poor Laws and Relief of Distress through Unemployment was made enjoyable by the attention and attractions of two women who fought politely and at some verbal distance from one another for the minds if not the hearts of their assistants. The Barnetts, the Bosanquets, the Webbs, the Hammonds, and the Coles are outstanding examples of double-starred personalities who have thrown light upon the dark places of English urban and rural poverty. They have all been conspicuous for their energetic earnestness, scorn of display, and passion for social betterment. Miss Octavia Hill was a member of the Poor Law Commission, but I saw nothing of her. Helen Dendy, at 35, had married Bernard Bosanquet, ' the philosopher of reality as the absolute.' She had translated Sigwart's *Logic* and become a district secretary of the Charity Organisation Society. Beatrice Potter had also worked off and on for some years for this Society as a young woman. She had also gone rent collecting in some ' model ' buildings and worked as a trouser-hand in tailoring workshops in East London. At 34 she married Sidney Webb, a former Civil Servant, eighteen months her

junior. Two years earlier they had attended a Co-operative Con-
gress in Glasgow and " with glory in the sky and hideous bestiality
on the earth" had made a working compact which was to issue in
joined and dedicated lives for more than half a century. " I am a
piece of steel " she warned her admiring suitor. " One and one
placed close together" he retorted in the sort of love-letter to be
expected from one whose favourite reading had been *Kelly's
Directory* " in a sufficiently integrated relationship make not two
but eleven." During their courtship contrary to expectation he
had not read a Blue Book to her but he had read Keats and Rossetti.
Helen Bosanquet and Beatrice Webb were both good and able
women. Their relationship brings to mind the couplet :
> "The good are so harsh to the clever
> The clever so rude to the good."

One may have been nearer to the simplicity and transparency of
mind which we associate with goodness. Each pursued the truth,
if not at all costs, but their researches led to opposed programmes of
social action. Nor were their views fundamentally changed by
listening to witnesses whose evidence filled the closely printed
columns of forty-seven volumes. One signed the Majority Report
and the other the Minority Report. Mrs. Bosanquet was the less
clever and the more honest-in-the-grain of the two ; Mrs. Webb the
more humorous and the greater charmer. These were the years of
" her most Machiavellian efforts." Professor Smart, who was
nothing if not orthodox and conventional, was scared of her. She
possessed what Mrs. Hamilton calls " that higher kind of un-
scrupulousness which belongs to every effective driving personality."[1] With a curve of her voice and a wave of her hand she
swept you into her net and you found she was surreptitiously
preparing to dismember the Poor Law limb from limb and that

[1] *Sidney and Beatrice Webb.* By M. A. Hamilton. P. 189.

Sidney was already secretly drafting a report in that sense to be launched simultaneously with that of the Majority.   The homes of the two women were refined and orderly, each displaying a disciplined taste which showed no trace of careless feminine abandon in Bond Street or the Rue de Rivoli.   No child's voice broke the silence of the study either at Oxted or Passfield Corner.

There were three Principals in my time at Glasgow : John Caird, Robert Herbert Story, and Donald MacAlister.   Caird was a pulpit orator and whenever he was announced to preach in the Bute Hall or a city church, Williams and I would be there.   His doctrine was broader than the creeds ... " Every man who desires to do good," I heard him proclaim, "is an ordained priest."   Story had a reputation as an ecclesiastical controversialist with a gift for acid and scornful comment, and none of the diplomatic arts of his successor.   We were unaware that his grave appearance concealed unusual powers of mimicry.   When the other day I saw a self-portrait of Camille Pissarro, with his flowing beard, I was reminded of Story.[1]   He was the only Principal I have known who came to listen to juniors like myself lecture to students in the ordinary class. I was at once flattered and a trifle embarrassed at this mark of interest and encouragement.   I saw more of MacAlister who ruled the University for twenty-two years, and then followed Rosebery as Chancellor.   He filled the years with his swift and abounding energy in Glasgow, and in London where for twenty-seven years he was President of the General Medical Council.   While he talked with you he wrote at the same time the briefest letters of business or friendship, concealing beneath his brisk efficient manner a kindly, even affectionate nature.   But, it was said, if you wished to circumvent him in any of his set policies you would have to get up early and sit up late.   He was every inch a Highlander.

* * * * * * *

[1] *Letters to his son, Lucien.*   P. 337.

In the eighteen eighties there lived in the Russian town of Bielstok, on the Polish border, a young man who was worried by the existence side-by-side of the languages of Russians, Poles, Germans and Jews. By the time he was nineteen he had thought out the grammar and vocabulary of a new international language. In 1887 he published it at his own expense under the title : *An International Language by Dr. Esperanto, Preface and Full Manual.* This pseudonym which means " he who is hoping " became the name of the language itself and its familiar vocabulary, phonetic spelling and regular grammer attracted to it many students and among them Dr. R. J. Lloyd, my wife's polyglottic father. In an article in the *Westminster Review* (December, 1903,) he made a detailed comparison of Esperanto and English and argued that it would cost a foreigner several times more time and trouble to attain competent knowledge of English than to attain an equally competent knowledge of Esperanto. Existing languages are all considerably irregular and illogical. Esperanto is neither and this simplification meant immense economy of effort.

High hopes of the new invention were held fifty years ago by many besides Dr. Lloyd, but mankind is governed by sentiment no less than by economics. As I write these lines the Indian Assembly has decided that English shall remain the official language of India for fifteen years, after which it is to be replaced by Hindi. Mr. Nehru pointed out to the Assembly : " English to-day is far more important to the world than it was when the British came here." I have been present at Cabinet meetings at which Indian Maharajahs could understand each other only by using English.

In August, 1906, Esperantists from many nations met in conference at Geneva under the leadership of their founder, Dr. Zamenhof. To this gathering went Dr. R. J. Lloyd, and his youngest daughter, Lilian. On Wednesday, August 29, Dr. and

Miss Lloyd, after an Esperantist luncheon, took a walk along the banks of the Arve towards its junction with the Rhone. Near the junction, Dr. Lloyd wrote a long letter to his wife and seemed quite self-possessed. As they advanced the footpath became more difficult to follow and about 6 p.m.Dr. Lloyd scrambled up some dangerous cliffs and disappeared in the bushes and trees with which the bank was covered. He was soon out of sight and did not return. After some days his body was found in the Rhone. What accident befell him and how he came by his death remain a mystery.

Richard John Lloyd who thus paid the penalty of a life of excessive mental concentration was no ordinary person. His Welsh ancestors had been tenant farmers of the same land for centuries at Maesgwyn, on the Chirk Castle estate of the Myddleton-Biddulphs, Denbighshire, and are mentioned in the report of the Welsh Land Commission.[1] Local tradition said they had been tenants from around 1300. At some stage in their history they had followed the Wesleys and become ardent Methodists. They married Methodists : Crombies, Chadwicks, Hockings, Rigbys and Snapes. But the last of the long line of farming tenants, William Lloyd, who died in 1937, had been a pillar of the parish church, had read the lessons for fifty years and for twenty-one years had served in the Denbighshire Hussars, retiring with the rank of sergeant-major.

An earlier Lloyd, John (1789-1855), had migrated to Liverpool, and in April, 1822, had founded a family firm of port gaugers with, later, branches at Hull and Goole, which lasted a hundred years. It was an ancient office to which the holders were appointed by the grand jury at Quarter Sessions, after taking an elaborate oath. An Act of 1531, connected with the assizes of bread and ale, had directed that the Warden of the Mystery of Coopers should take the gauge of all barrels offered for sale. Apparently a barrel could not

[1] C7757, Q. 55, 100 (1895).

be used until certified by the Warden.   The gauger's duty was, by
means of certain instruments and calculations, to check the quantities, in casks of imported wines, spirits and oils.   His certificate
was conclusive as between buyer and seller.

John was succeeded by a nephew Richard in 1855.   It is in his
son that we are interested.   In 1866, when twenty, Richard John
had been a successful candidate for the Indian Civil Service, but
being an only son and devoted to his mother he did not take up the
post assigned to him in Bengal.   He joined the family firm of port
gaugers, and spent his life in Liverpool.   Scholarship had an
irresistible attraction for him and he grew into "a phantom of texture midway between life and books."   Arber, Sweet and Hales had
been his examiners, and Arber declared that Lloyd was unsurpassed
in his line of study by any other of his generation.   This line was
phonetics.   Lloyd had more than immense industry.   Murray of
the Oxford Dictionary considered Lloyd's essay on Phonetic Attraction a most important piece of original work, and Vietor of Marburg,
' did not hesitate to signalize' the treatises on "Vowel-Sounds and
Speech Sounds" as marking a new epoch in the science of Phonetics.
So they testified when Lloyd was a candidate for the post of Principal at Aberystwyth in 1891.   Scholarship, however, is not the
only qualification required in a Principal.   Lloyd became Honorary
Reader in Phonetics at the University of Liverpool and carried on
with his gauging.   He served as a member of the School Board,
and was a promoter of special schools for the mentally deficient.
It was a life of unwearied industry maintained unbroken for forty
years and ending in the tragedy not of a deficient but of an excessive
and over-taxed intellect.   The University Senate recorded the loss
of a scholar " as exceptional in attainments as in modesty."

Dr. Lloyd was a quiet unobtrusive man of fixed abstemious
habits, somewhat deaf, well and carefully dressed, inclined to be

absent-minded in small matters. I never established relations of easy intercourse with him ; he had no small talk in English and I could supply him with no linguistic exchange or exercise in any of the many European languages in which he was fluent. He was twice married and had four children. Neither wife was the perfect companion—if such there could ever be—of a student who required domestic silence from six to ten every evening, having been in business all day. No one worked more methodically. He was a Victorian father to his children and spared no effort to provide them with the best education within reach of his modest means. My contribution to the family happiness was to rescue the second daughter, Eirene, from an excessive desire to please her father by pursuing academic distinctions at Aberystwyth, London, Cambridge and Paris. Accounts had been strictly kept and she was glad to repay him what he had spent on her college education. Her relation to him had been one of deep respect rather than love.

* * * * * * * *

In the course of 1909 I was sounded about various appointments : an Associate Professorship in Toronto, a Chair in Economics in Sheffield, and the Principalship of Ruskin College, Oxford. As the next section will show it was to Queen's University, Belfast, that I decided to go.

Before I cross the channel—I am certain to be sea-sick—I must lighten this sober chronicle with some reference to the recreations we enjoyed in Glasgow. I played no games but, as I have said, preferred to sleep in the afternoons ; to reach the country even in a tramcar took too much time. On a day of sunshine I might join a Welsh student of divinity and saunter along Sauchiehall Street assigning classes and marks for good looks to the women shoppers.

Much later I learnt that Sir Francis Galton followed our practice when collecting materials for a Beauty Map of the British Isles. He classified the girls he passed in the streets or elsewhere as attractive, indifferent, or repellent. He found London to rank highest for beauty, Aberdeen lowest. Richard Jones and I were less scientific in our perambulations and kept no records.[1]

Once R. R. Williams and I took up a challenge to attract and hold a crowd on Glasgow Green in competition with the other compellers of attention. At this time I knew a lot about Poland and we passed ourselves off as Polish refugees, speaking broken English with our native accent, and when I was through with my speech and had referred to the fact that " all our songs are in the minor key " I called on the tenor at my side to sing one of the most moving of our Welsh melodies. The effect was electrical and so successful that we decided to withdraw before taking a collection. On this occasion we had warned in Welsh any countryman present not to give us away as a bet was at stake.

But much the best relaxation was to be found in the generous hospitality of the homes of our Scottish fellow-students at the week-ends or bank-holidays down the Clyde. I vividly recall wonderful afternoon teas at Kilmalcolm, Kames, Colintraive and Tighnahbruaich, and even more wonderful psalm-singing on Sundays:

> " Ye whales that in the waters move
> Your Maker's praises spout ;
> Ye codfish on the banks that leap
> And lash your tails about."

Fares were low—3/9d. return rail and steamer to Brodick in Arran, and you could walk round the island for nothing. I never did, holding that the value of such exercise is exaggerated, but I washed the feet of Kenneth Leys who tramped the fifty odd miles in a day,

---

[1] Galton : *Memories of my Life* (1908). P. 315.

when he arrived back proud and tired at the cottage in Glen Sherraig in the gloaming.

On a Sunday morning we would walk to Brodick church to hear Mr. Maclean preach a fine sermon, albeit with a snuffle, on the wisdom of passivity, for example, from the text " Except the Lord build the house." Through the two western windows we saw the blue sky and the bare fir branches, and heard the thrushes singing joyfully outside while inside we sang about " this perplexing path of life " and our wandering footsteps therein. Then homewards to Miss Fullarton's cottage up the glen, observing the sprouting prim-roses and daffodils and the faint but distinct hint of green in the larches, while the stream ran warmer and to one's feeling more freely and blissfully in the spring weather.

* * * * * * * *

In June, 1922, I went back to Glasgow to receive the honorary degree of Doctor of Laws. The news of this had come to me some weeks earlier as a complete and thrilling surprise. William Temple, Louis Raemakers, and Eleutherios Venizelos replied for the graduates at the luncheon which followed the capping ceremony. After chaffing Glasgow and Cambridge, Temple talked of Balliol under the Mastership of Edward Caird and described a scene not without its parallel at Aberystwyth in my time. There were certain functions, said the Archbishop, in which Caird involved the students, when they used to go, about a dozen at a time, and stand on one side of the drawing-room, while an exactly equal number of young ladies used to come and stand on the other side. There they stood in two stiff rows and in grim silence until it was announced that breakfast was ready, and when they got into the dining-room they found that the alternate seats were occupied by the ladies, to whom they were intro-duced and were expected to keep up necessary conversation through-out the meal. The Master did not always furnish an admirable example.   He used to sit in silence gazing at the ceiling, presumably in communion with the Absolute, and when the breakfast was finished he would exclaim to the young lady on his right hand, " I detest motor cars."   She would say anxiously—" Oh, yes," and the conversation lapsed.   On some occasions, marvellous as his teaching was, he used to baffle their inquiries.   Temple remembered a lecturer who was puzzled between the determinism apparently involved in the Master's logic and the theory of freedom involved in his ethics, and asked him how that was so, and what on his theory happened when one chose to do something, to which the Master replied in those glorious words—" I presume that the universe concentrates itself upon the individual."   " Oh," said the lecturer, and that conversation also lapsed.

There were similar stories about Caird in Glasgow.   He used to invite the best students to breakfast after the eight o'clock class, and after breakfast took them out for a walk.   One friend of mine had this experience.   In the course of the walk Caird made only one remark, about some building they passed, and he repeated it on the way home.   The perfect Caird story is that of Mrs. Caird discovering him standing beside his bath in the early morning : " Am I going in or am I coming out?"

II

IRELAND 1905—1910

I was appointed Professor in Economics at Queen's University, Belfast, in the summer of 1909 but my stay there was brief. This was not my first introduction to Ireland, with whose affairs I have been concerned at more than one stage of my life. As early as 1904, while still resident in Glasgow, I became a peripatetic lecturer in Ireland, a post which brought me in contact with Irish audiences in towns and villages throughout the country. As Barrington Lecturer the opportunity came my way of seeing something of the Irish problem at close quarters, an experience which was to prove useful in later days. I was able as a Welshman to assess in some measure the magnitude of Anglo-Saxon blunders in dealing with Ireland. It is a melancholy story and one from which the English not unnaturally turn their eyes. It led to a series of tragedies which better statesmanship would have averted and for which the unleashing of elemental passions in Ireland must also be held largely responsible. It is a story not without its moral for Wales.

* * * * * * *

"We have more to do with Ireland than with all the world besides," declared James I and this was almost always true in peace and in war down to 1938, when Britain accepted the Irish Constitution which had replaced that of the Irish Free State, and when on the 6th of May of that year the first President of Ireland was elected. The war followed in 1939 and with her neutrality and strict censorship, Eire isolated herself and only rarely disturbed the current of our politics. Englishmen knew little and cared less about what was happening across the Channel outside Northern Ireland. We had enough to do " with all the world besides " and little to do with Eire—in complete contrast with the history of the preceding centuries.

Writing in the early eighteen eighties, Matthew Arnold spoke of the two peoples as *The Incompatibles* : as the years proceeded it appeared that *The Irreconcilables* would have been a truer character-isation. Ireland has furnished only one example, if the nearest to us, of the deadly destructiveness of the idea of political nationalism, which has soaked Europe in blood, and wherever it has gone has given rise to the most amazing manifestations of intolerance, hatred, cruelty and terrorism. All these methods of barbarism, raised to the nth power by the mechanical resources of civilization, were to be displayed by the two neighbours in the half century which followed the ' sweetness and light' of *Irish Essays*.

In 1836, George Cornewall Lewis described Ireland as having been for the preceding seventy years the scene of recurring insurrection. Successive governments had loaded the statute book with the severest laws, covered the country with military and police, inflicted capital punishment unsparingly : and all to no purpose. The fifty years which followed 1836 wrought little change for the better and added the terrors of secret societies operating from the security of America. At last a great statesman and orator endowed with superhuman energy, grappled with the intractable problem and advanced a measure which to-day bears all the marks of a modest and reasonable compromise. It laid down five essential conditions : unity of empire, political equality, equitable distribution of imperial burdens, protection of minorities ; the fifth was that the measure should present the essential character of a settlement.

All have vanished. It was the last chance given to England to fix the floating, warring elements of the Irish nation into a constitutional and imperial pattern acceptable to the majority and containing some hope of permanence. The rejection of Mr. Gladstone's Home Rule Bill in 1886 was one of England's greatest political blunders and the parent of innumerable crimes and misfortunes. It was a major disaster comparable with the failure of the Normans, eight centuries earlier, to dominate Ireland and impose their civilization upon it.

No one who was an adolescent in the eighteen eighties, however ignorant, could escape being drawn into the controversy ; the subject occupied more of the time of parliament and the space of newspapers than any other. In Wales, where Mr. Gladstone paradoxically was the nonconformist hero, it dominated all topics of conversation. The Welshman's love of liberty and toleration was stronger than his hatred of Roman Catholicism, and Home Rule was supported wholeheartedly by twenty-six out of thirty Welsh members of parliament. The affinity of the two languages provided a bond of interest among a small band of scholars, but the two countries differed deeply in national and religious tradition. In Ireland feuds rarely ceased, even monasteries fought among themselves, long before it was to become " the isle of bullets, beads and bombs." In Wales, for many centuries past, bishops and ministers had recourse to no more deadly weapon than the tongue, the tract, or an anonymous magazine article. We are intemperate and inflammable, but neither boycotters nor moonlighters ; neither cruel nor murderous, but slanderous within the bounds of the law and compromisers in the gate. Our Chartist risings, Rebecca and tithe riots, our passive resistance were rosewater rebellions and exceptional not endemic. Our law courts are so free of crime that another name for the Land of My Fathers is the Land of White Gloves. Latterly, in 1936, it is true, we have seen in Wales a bombing school fired in protest against English domination and " in obedience to conscience and the moral law" but this aberration has not, so far, been followed.

My first holiday, paid for with my own savings of a few pounds, in the summer of 1888, was spent with a fellow-clerk on the North Wales coast, with Rhyl as base, in a small temperance hotel. There were trips to Hawarden, where we just missed seeing Mr. Gladstone felling trees, and to Bangor where I first saw Henry Jones, and heard him lecture on *Excelsior*. Our most venturesome journey was to Dublin, attracted thither by a Tredegar friend employed in the Irish Land Commission. He had arranged that we should stay at the Northumberland Hotel, which had a Welsh landlord, named Lewis. We had been so sick and battered during the rough crossing from Holyhead that we had fallen asleep across a table in a stuffy cabin crowded with cattledealers and were wakened by a Welsh steward after the boat had been some time in dock. Outside it was raining hard. We hailed a side-car and asked to be taken to the Northumberland Hotel. "Sure," said the driver, "there's no such place in all Ireland; I'll drive ye to the Hibernian Hotel." After many remonstrances he said at last, "Jump up, and I'll try and find it," He drove straight to our hotel and greeted Mr. Lewis : " These young Welshmen wanted to go to the Hibernian, so I told them to come here to their own countryman." During our short visit we went to a service at the Welsh Presbyterian chapel in Talbot Street, frequented by Holyhead sailors, and to Phoenix Park where we drew our sticks along the cross in the turf which marked the site of the murder of Lord Frederick Cavendish and Thomas Henry Burke. My appetite for social facts was already active for I remember, during this visit, asking the driver of a jaunting-car what was the chief ambition of young Irishmen and being told " Sure, to be an Inspector." Later I was to discover that being priests, publicans, policemen and politicians also appealed to the aspiring youth of Ireland.

It was 1904 before I again went to Ireland. I was then a junior lecturer in Glasgow and noticed in one of the weeklies that a man was required by the Barrington Trust to lecture on Political Economy in the towns and villages of Ireland, a part-time job which could perhaps be fitted in during the very long vacation of a Scottish University. Two hundred guineas were offered for fifty lectures. I knew nothing whatever of the Barrington Trust but I applied and some weeks later received a long telegram requesting me to appear on a certain date in the Molesworth Hall, Dublin, and be ready to speak for twenty minutes on Free Trade and Protection, a subject which Joseph Chamberlain had recently made alive in his tariff reform campaign. In due course I walked into the Molesworth Hall and found about a hundred men and women assembled, some in evening dress and all belonging to the professional classes. The chief trustee, Richard M. Barrington, welcomed me and introduced me to the chairman of the meeting, R. E. Matheson, Registrar-General of Ireland. I was told that four out of the thirty-three candidates had been chosen to speak that evening and that I would be called up last. I settled down to listen to the other three. The first, a graduate of the Royal University, was blessed with a strong Irish brogue but cursed with too many notes for his short speech. He was for protection. The next was a highly refined product of Trinity College and he tabulated a catalogue of $\times$ arguments for Free Trade and $\times + 1$ or 2 arguments for Protection. The third was a much more formidable candidate, spoke persuasively without notes in an attractive manner, and came down heavily on the Free Trade side. We had been charged to have in mind not the audience before us but a typical village gathering. I sensed that the audience before us was divided in opinion and that it was a mistake to dogmatize on such a controversial issue. It was wiser to expound the nature of trade in general and add the modifications attributable to the opposing views in an expository style. When I sat down all could understand the difference but no one could say to which party I belonged, which seemed to me the right method for a teacher. I was appointed. At the end of the meeting I was introduced to the third speaker. He was H. B. Lees-Smith, then Vice-Principal of Ruskin College, Oxford, and subsequently Postmaster General, President of the Board of Education, and a Cabinet Minister in the Labour Government of 1929-1931.

A family named Barrington settled in Queen's County, Ireland, in the second half of the sixteenth century. A descendent named John Barrington (1800-1836) by his will bequeathed the sum of £3,000, in trust, the interest to be applied " for the payment of a fit and proper person, duly qualified to give lectures on Political Economy in its most extended and useful sense, but particularly as relates to the conduct and duty of people to one another, these lectures to be given in the various town and villages of Ireland, without distinction and as often as may be."

The early eighteen-thirties, as we have seen, were years of tithe wars and coercion acts, accompanied by violence and outrage. John Barrington in his business as a maker of soap and candles, was troubled in his short life by sympathetic strikes and doubtless hoped by his bequest to lessen the strife between employers and workmen. The fund was allowed to accumulate and in the early part of 1849 the Trustees requested the Council of the Statistical and Social Inquiry Society of Ireland to assist them in selecting lecturers. From that time onwards there have been many Barrington lecturers who became eminent as lawyers and economists, a Master of the Rolls, and a Lord Chancellor among the former, Hearn, Cairnes,

Cliffe Leslie, J. K. Ingram, and Bastable among the latter. My immediate predecessor was Professor C. H. Oldham, Dean of the Faculty of Commerce in the National University of Ireland, who proved most hospitable and helpful. The Contemporary Club met at his house on Saturday nights for coffee, and there one encountered a curious mixture of professors, poets, government officials, wits and cranks, all brilliant talkers and eager for an audience. I learnt much from them.

My other mentor was the acting trustee, Richard Manliffe Barrington (1849-1915). He was the eighth and youngest son of Edward, brother of the John already mentioned. He was a gentleman farmer living at Fassaroe, near Bray in County Wicklow, and a casual passer-by might easily have mistaken him for a country labourer. He was in fact one of the best educated men I have ever known. He was a barrister and knew law ; a land-valuer and knew economics ; a botanist who knew the ways of plants ; an ornithologist who knew the ways of birds ; a successful farmer who could produce his own and his father's accounts for every field and animal for half a century. With all this knowledge and true to his Quaker origins he avoided publicity, quietly supported the leading learned societies, and never used two words where one would do. To walk with him over his fields was humiliating—he saw so much that his companion missed. ' Do you see those birds ? They are on their way to Iceland. They usually pass this way during this week.' ' Look at this slender plant. It is the Dodder (*Cuscuta trifolii*), hard to find.' When he was 23 he was quoted as an authority for new localities of plants in as many as six counties. He had a great reputation among Alpine climbers and in 1882, in a stormy and unpropitious summer, he ascended within eleven days the Schreckhorn, Finsteraahorn, Jungfrau and Matterhorn, with an equal number of high passes, making in all a record of 84,500 feet within that brief period.[1]   For nearly twenty years he visited the remotest islands from St. Kilda to the Blaskets, living on them for days and weeks at a time in the height of the breeding season.   From 1886 he had an arrangement with the keepers of Irish lighthouses and lightships by which the legs and wings of birds found blown to death were labelled and sent to him.   At Fassaroe they were preserved and arranged in chests of narrow drawers and the data carefully noted and presently published in his large book *The Migration of Birds*.[2]

When I add that Richard Barrington was blessed with a handsome and highly intelligent and humorous wife, Lena Gyles of County Waterford, whom he married in 1897, it will be understood that my friendship with the Barringtons added compound interest to the monetary rewards of the Barrington Lecturer.

The old Glasgow session ended in March so I was able to fit in my quota of lectures in the Christmas vacations, the early spring and the late autumn.   R. M. B. bade me not neglect the villages for the towns and not to mind the small audiences.   I chose a centre in which to reside for a month and visited the villages within a radius of twenty or thirty miles, giving short courses of three or four lectures on successive Mondays, Tuesdays and so forth. Oldham had warned me that I should have to choose the villages, book halls, issue posters, find chairmen, boost myself and supply press reports. This was no light matter and much of it devolved on my methodical wife who dealt with letters at headquarters.   In arranging preliminaries I began with whoever corresponded to a Town Clerk and found out from him all about the leading figures in the churches, schools and shops.   Care had to be taken to keep a right balance

---

[1] C. B. Moffat : *The Irish Naturalist*.   Nov. 1915.
[2] R.M.B. bequeathed the collection to The Natural History Museum, Dublin, with a sum of money for its care and maintenance.

between Catholic and Protestant as chairmen of my meetings. Fortunately there existed a Barrington tradition and my appearance was never resented and was usually cordially welcomed. My most distinguished chairman was at Armagh, in the person of Cardinal Logue, the bilingual son of a Donegal innkeeper. He invited me after the lecture to sup with him on champagne and oysters, while his young chaplain sipped a glass of milk. In view of my Welsh nonconformist abstinence it was jocularly agreed that His Eminence should pronounce the champagne to be milk.

During my tenure of the lectureship I must have spoken in forty of fifty places scattered over the four provinces. For head-quarters I often chose small seaside towns : Rostrevor, Tramore, Kilkee, Bundoran, Portstewart. At Tramore, my wife and I went from the Grand Hotel with the Countess Mountcashell to see a company of strolling players perform *Hamlet*. We found we were the only adults in the bare and bleak hall, the rest of the audience being a score of school-children. After a long wait the leading actor came forward to announce that the company felt they could not, before such a meagre audience, do justice to the great tragedy ; they would instead recite selected passages from the works of Shakespeare for our edification. This they did and I tendered our thanks.

Long years before the days of Arthur Griffith or Mr. de Valera, Dean Swift had drawn up a *Proposal for the Universal Use of Irish Manufacture* and commanded the ladies never to appear arrayed in a single shred from England. " Burn everything English except her coals." On the Strand at Kilkee we lived in a cottage belonging to descendants of Gerald Griffin and it was recommended to us as being furnished with the maximum number of articles made in Ireland. I remember going to it from Mount Trenchard, Foynes, the house of the Monteagles, where my room had figured draperies, chair covers and curtains designed by William Morris. The cottage and the mansion had a common feeling for beauty but were at different levels of achievement.

Audiences varied from forty or fifty to two or three hundred. I recall the titles of some of the lectures : Emigration and Agriculture, Education and Industry, Protection of Native Industries, Democracy, Unemployment. I stuck as closely as possible to Economics and steered clear of party politics. At the close of each lecture, discussion and questions followed and it was then I learnt how true it was that Irish history was for Englishmen to remember and for Irishmen to forget. One speaker after another would wander back to the golden age of Irish religion, art and literature in the seventh century and point me to the Book of Kells as proof of what unaided the uncorrupted Irishmen could do. The Catholic would sneer at Belfast as only able to make collars, cuffs, and cigarettes ; the Protestant at Dublin as a city of clerks and dressmakers. One critic would curse the statue of Cromwell at Westminster or the Plantation of Ulster, another denounce England for destroying Irish industries in the eighteenth century. The appeal to the Irish of the past excused all faults in the Irish of the present. We are still told that " One must know what Spenser said in 1596 before one can say the last word on the most recent riot in the Abbey Theatre."[1] At a lecture in Dublin on Trade Unionism, Oldham took the chair and ruled out of order questions on Socialism to the annoyance of the hecklers. When I rose to move a vote of thanks to him for presiding about thirty of the audience walked out as a protest. But this was an exceptional experience and usually I contrived to avoid extreme displays of disagreement. Once a speaker closed the argument with the admission " If we are an island of saints we are the divil's own saints."

* * * * * * *

[1] Don Byrne : *I remember Karrigeen* (1944). P. 87.

What did I know of the people I had been appointed to instruct in the elements of political economy ? Not much. I had been brought up in the Gladstonian Home Rule tradition and I had listened in Rhymney to eloquent Irish Nationalist M.P.s dilate on the wrongs of Ireland, and I had read Lever's *Charles O'Malley* in a sixpenny reprint. At Aberystwyth I had read Spenser on the state of Ireland in the 16th century as a set book for a London Inter-mediate examination, and retained a vague recollection of the poet's description of a country given over to lawlessness and savagery. And I was familiar with the contrasted picture of a romantic Ireland drawn by Thomas Davis, who, it should be remembered, was only thirty when he died. I had the intuitive sympathy of a Welshman for a small nation struggling to be free and none of the inveterate sentiment of hostility flavoured with contempt which Mr. Gladstone once described as characteristic of the feeling of Englishmen towards Ireland. The opposed and typical attitude towards the English was revealed to me by almost the first Irishman I met in Dublin : " You are all too busy making money to trouble about Hindoos and Irishmen." We certainly have had trouble enough since with both. This notion of a prosperous England entirely given over to a mater-ialistic imperialism was in 1904 part of the aftermath of the South African war, but it is also part of the envy engendered in many countries by our having been ahead of them in launching the In-dustrial Revolution. " Sie haben den grossen Geldbeutel " one frequently heard in Germany. It is a recurring theme with Irish writers. Moira O'Neill sings :

" The people that's in England is richer nor the Jews,
There's not the smallest young gossoon but travels in his shoes !"

J. B. Yeats in his letters cannot long keep away from attempts to sum up the contrasts between the two countries. Thus he writes

to his son : " Spite is to Ireland what selfishness is to England : the
the first is barbarism—the other civilization, *such as it is*.   Spite is
an entirely disinterested desire to destroy success wherever you see
it.   Selfishness likes success for therein it sees some opportunity for
itself."[1]

Politically I was no further to the Left of the Centre than was
implied in membership of the Fabian Society.   I had in full measure
the antipathy of a Welsh Calvinistic Methodist to Roman Catholicism, and even to-day with all the toleration and self-knowledge of
advancing years I am filled with distrust when I learn that the
Foreign Office and the B.B.C. harbour a disproportionate number of
Romans in the ranks of the higher officials.   I prefer a disproportion
of Protestants.

In 1890 a Fellow of All Souls, Sir Thomas Raleigh, writing on
Irish politics laid down three rules to be observed by those who
wished to form a sound opinion on the Irish Question :

  1. Read Thom's Directory and other works of a merely
       statistical character.
  2. See the country for yourself, independently, and not
       under the personal conduct of any Irish partisan.
  3. Do not believe any story which tells against an individual
       (landlord or tenant, official or agitator) until you have
       considered carefully what the person accused has to say
       for himself.

I tried to follow Raleigh's advice.   I bought a 1903 Directory.
I consulted the experts of " the Department," T. P. Gill, the
Secretary, and George Adams, later Warden of All Souls, who then
rejoiced in the office and title of Superintendent of Statistics and
Intelligence. I possessed myself of a volume describing Irish in-
dustries with statistics and maps, issued by " the Department" :

---

[1] *Letters.*   P. 158.

Ireland Industrial and Agricultural, the first evidence of a conscious policy of developing the resources of Ireland as a whole, undertaken by the officers of a government which, one Irishman told me, had for seven hundred years done nothing but ignore what they did not penalise. Sir Horace Plunkett had given offence to the Tories by appointing Gill, a nationalist, and by importing Scotsmen to teach the Irish. Adams was one of these. Another was James Wilson, Professor of Agriculture in the Royal College, who had come to Dublin from Aberdeen, via Aberystwyth, and from him I learnt something of the importance of the cow in the Irish national economy.

Plunkett, whom I was to meet often in years to come, looked upon creameries as his children and when one was threatened with financial breakdown he moved heaven and earth to keep it going, whereas it might have been better to let it sink as a warning to others. This mischief began when the Irish Agricultural Organisation Society published dotted maps showing its successes and betrayed too great an eagerness for quick results.

The horse was important in the social and economic life of Ireland and there was an export trade to South America. I remember on the morning of the local races going into the public reading room in Limerick and seeing a procession of young men passing through after making notes from the sporting columns. But the horse was not to be compared with the cow. Store cattle were sent from Ireland to be fattened in the eastern strip from Lincolnshire to Forfar, where they were stall fed in winter. This enabled the farmers of that strip to till more land. A good Scottish ploughman would drive the plough seven inches deep and seven or eight inches wide, where the Irish ploughman would go four inches deep and ten inches wide, leaving beneath a hard pan, unbroken for ages, never facing the light, and needing now much more power to break through it. The treatment of calves in Aberdeen and Ireland was very different, so Wilson told me. In the former a calf six or seven months old would be worth £8 or £10 ; in Ireland £5. Fed with milk from birth, it would fetch £18 to £22 when just under two years old, whereas the starved Irish calves would only fetch half these figures. In Aberdeen the calf was put indoors in September or October and from then on added £1 per month to its value, when the Irish calf would add a fourth of this through the winter. There was much high argument on the merits of keeping and fattening the cow in Ireland. If fresh meat could be carried from Glasgow to London by water, could it not be carried from Navan to Liverpool ? By slaughtering at home employment would be found in producing by-products of bone, hoof, and horn. The cows' hair had a market value for plasterers, and thus various industries were at hand without going more than skin deep into the cow.

T. W. Lyster, of the National Library, was another who put my feet on the road to knowedge of Ireland. He was overwhelmingly kind and enthusiastic at the arrival of a new learner. He gave me half an hour of breathless attention, leading me along the galleries, bidding me read this and avoid that work, apologising for a book he found misplaced by a careless reader or a tired assistant. The books were minutely classified, e.g. for free trade, against free trade. I was given a table at the end of the Economics Gallery, furnished with pens, ink, blotting paper, and a clean duster. I was introduced to the Chief Assistant and several juniors so that they might thereafter recognize my face in the building as that of a trustworthy reader. I had no words of thanks left. I read Blue Books from the fat folio of the Devon Commission, 1845, to the widely-quoted and influential report of the Childers Commission on the financial relations of Great Britain and Ireland, 1896. I did not read all the Blue Books, as their number was legion.

I obeyed Raleigh's second injunction and saw the country for myself. It was a sharp change of social climate to travel direct from highly industrialized Glasgow to the primitive easy-going half-barbarous villages of the West of Ireland or its small provincial towns asleep in the long afternoons. I had to beware of applying the principles of political economy in all their unmitigated severity to Donegal and Connemara, or expecting to find there the rhythmic harmonies of the law of supply and demand. To cross even to the east coast from Glasgow to a village on Carlingford Lough, was in many ways to leave the twentieth century behind for the seventeenth. There you were either a Protestant or a Papist and everybody knew which. The village was split in two. You shopped according to creed rather than quality or price. Your landlady whispered, as you went out, that Mr. A. was a Protestant chemist and you might trust him not to poison you. The charwoman, however, was a Catholic and so was the maid-servant. But around Carlingford Lough you were on the Border, where, forty years ago, sectarian feeling ran high. Indeed the village which I have in mind was proclaimed by Government and you might not play the *Boyne Water* or *The Wearing of the Green* on a concertina or a penny whistle unless you wished to be pounced upon by two—they always went in twos—of the dozen policemen who guarded the village of 660 souls.

Away from the Border, miles away from Orange drums and Green banners, the parish priest was willing to preside at your lecture and the Episcopal clergyman or the Presbyterian doctor to propose a vote of thanks to you. Wherever I lectured I called on the priest of the parish and though there were degrees of cordiality I was never repelled. I was struck with the plain simplicity, the bareness of the Presbytery. There were few books in evidence, in marked contrast with the excellent libraries of the majority of Welsh nonconformist ministers. The lower fringe of the clerical

order was obviously drawn from the peasantry and had undergone
a certain amount of smoothing and ironing in a seminary. I was
told that the level of culture and manners amongst the younger
priests was falling and that this was due to the lower social strata
from which they were increasingly recruited. " There is not a
gentleman among them," remarked Lady Fingall. The older
generation of priests were genial, tolerant and helpful, obtruded
neither their politics nor their theology upon the visitors. I may
have been treading on mines, but they did not explode.

My visits as Barrington Lecturer coincided with a period of
comparative tranquillity. " Ireland," Birrell declared in 1907, in a
sentence which he was never allowed to forget, " is in a more
peaceful condition than she has been for the last six hundred years."
What was the secret of this peaceful interlude ? Between 1903 and
1909 nearly 300,000 tenant cultivators were transformed into peasant
proprietors. The emigration safety-valve was still open and every
year 30,000 young men and women moved away to Britain and
America. The policy of violence was suspended and the urban
agitation of Larkin and Connolly had not yet broken out.

After making due allowance for Belfast's linen mills, shipyards
and tobacco factories, for Dublin's breweries and distilleries, and for
Limerick's bacon factories and Wexford's foundries, the cardinal
fact about Ireland is that it is mainly an agricultural country with
few other outlets for the industrial energies of the people. With all
its revolutions the island had escaped the one which most had
changed the face of England, the industrial. The manufactures of
Ireland have been abolished by the steam engines of England, wrote
T. H. Huxley.[1] Outside Dublin in 1926 there were in the Free State
ten towns each with a population above 10,000 and the highest of
these, Cork, was under 80,000.

[1] *The Coal Question* (1865). P. 203.

In the 18th century the commercial policy of England had damaged or destroyed one Irish industry after another, wool, glass, cotton. The trade in Irish beer, malt, hats, gunpowder, sails for the British navy, was restricted or stopped. This treatment was no isolated phenomenon but was the common practice of European countries towards their dependencies. Nursed by Grattan's parliament the infants revived, but when the Union consolidated the two countries, Irish industries, with the conspicuous exception of linen, could not withstand the competition of the more adult and robust manufactures of England and Scotland or, later, the bracing regimen of free trade.

During the last quarter of the 18th century, Irish corn enjoyed a preference in English ports over corn from foreign countries until the repeal of the English corn laws in 1846. This prosperity of the Irish grain trade had unfortunate results, partly owing to the custom of gavel kind. It led to an excessive subdivision of farms. The impecunious occupiers attracted a supply of cheap labour by letting off patches of ground on which peasants could build cabins and raise potatoes. This added to the number of cultivators competing with one another on the margin of existence, ignorant of the best methods of tillage, discouraged from trying them by rising rents, having no outlet for their energies but the land. When disease attacked the potato there was famine, not once nor twice— the great famine of the forties was but the climax of a series.[1]

The small holdings of this period with their dense population, have rightly been described as agricultural slums. In 1841, out of a total of 685,000 farms nearly five out of every six were of less than fifteen acres in extent. The situation slowly improved. In 1911 out of a total of 560,000 farms, 50,000 were of one to five acres : 130,000 five to fifteen : 120,000 fifteen to thirty. On many of these there

[1] See Murray : *Commercial Relations between England and Ireland.*

should never have been a rent charge. There was no surplus produce. I visited a rural parish ten miles by six which had not a
single plough in it. Rent on these holdings was a tax on wages,
wages often earned helping with the hay on English farms or Scottish
potato fields. Eighteen thousand labourers crossed the channel
every season from Connaught.

England's free trade policy gave an enormous stimulus to her
commerce for many years after the repeal of the corn laws. But
Ireland had no rapidly multiplying towns crying out for cheap food
and cheap clothing for her workers. The fiscal change took place
when Ireland was desolated by famine, death and emigration. For
some years Irish farmers were able to get high prices for meat, bacon
and butter. But with the revolution in ocean transport in the
seventies, Irish farmers, like our own, were severely hit.

The crushing out of Irish industries in earlier years, the absence
of towns and the stimulating competition they provide, the premium
put on laziness by landlords who raised rents to the tenants who
toiled and reduced them to tenants who loafed, the duty of keeping
up an appearance of squalor for the same reason and for the additional one that it afforded protection against a demand for an extra
church offering—these and other forces combined to discourage
thrift and industry, and perverted the orthodoxies of the text-books
of Political Economy.

There lingered also something of the influence of the reckless,
extravagant sporting landlord above the law rather than lawless,
and a love of noisy haggling over a bargain and the sealing of it in
the nearest public house. Behind this behaviour was a fundamental
clash of cultures. Lord Rosebery once asked if anyone had ever
heard of Wesleyans among the unemployed. Of course not. They
ran their religion on strictly business lines. Some contended that
Irish religious practice was not conducive to industrial success and

were asking how much religion a nation could stand without being ruined.   Many Irish thought of the world as made for contemplation and discourse and preferred to 'fleet the time carelessly as they did in the golden world.'. . Only for his dreams was a man responsible, wrote J. B. Yeats in a letter to his son : " Actions are a bastard race to which a man has not given his full paternity."[1]   In the west of Ireland man was one with nature.   " Man never obtrudes.   He is there : he is one of the live creatures : his house is made of the rock : his roof of the grass : he is dressed in colours of the hillsides : he never hurries or shouts ; he moves along with the rain, slow and patient and unabashed."   " These are the people who really look for the resurrection of the dead and the life of the world to come, and who look for little else."   A friend of mine asked Douglas Hyde, the President of the Gaelic League (later the President of Eire) to include the teaching of hygiene in the League programme and received for reply : The happiest homes I have known were the dirtiest.   And to this he added an Irish proverb : A hole is no disgrace, a patch is.

The countryside, it is true, was dotted with schools, but of the eight thousand, five thousand had only one room apiece, and of the seven hundred thousand children on the roll the average attendance was under five hundred thousand.   Half the children in the schools belonged to the infants class, and the majority of the rest left school after they had reached the third standard.   About one in twelve reached the highest standard.   Men teachers started with a salary of £52 per annum, women at £44.   Triennial increases of £7 brought an addition of £21 in nine years.   Critics at my lectures charged the English government with paying teachers small salaries in order to keep the Irish ignorant.

This was the people which Westminster had tried to bring up to

[1] *Letters.*   P. 189.

date, the human patient which had been dosed with forty Land
Acts, coercion, local government, twelve thousand policemen,
Agricultural Departments, royal visits, until the country resembled
an economic crèche. And the wisdom of Burke remained true :
concessions extorted from embarrassment and fear produce no
gratitude and allay no resentment.

* * * * * * *

A century ago Ireland had nearly three times as many in-
habitants as Scotland and half the population of England and Wales.
In the sixty years which followed the Famine the population fell
from something over 8 millions to less than 4½ millions, the great
majority being under ten and over forty-five years of age. Emigration became a habit so deeply rooted that children grew up intended
for the States. Everywhere in the west I found placards displaying
facilities for crossing the Atlantic. In a remote part of Donegal I
saw one of these large posters on a slab beside a little National
School. The first thing with which the child was made familiar
was an invitation to leave the country. And those who had gone
became the most active emigration agents for those left behind.
From a third to a half of those who crossed were said to do so in
response to a prepaid passage from the States. Side by side with
this movement had been a low marriage rate, a high birth rate, and
a high death rate. Dublin and Belfast around 1900 were notorious
for their death rates, those for young persons between 15 and 20
being much higher than the corresponding rates for a town like
Manchester. One reason for this was the prevalence of tuberculosis,
which having been reduced by nearly one half in forty years in
England and Scotland, was still obstinately high in Ireland. The
broad result to the eye of an economist was an enormous loss of
human capital. On the one hand Ireland was rearing boys and girls
on the land to the age of 18 or 20 and then exporting them as a gift

to America ; on the other hand, in the towns she was rearing boys
and girls to the age of 18 or 20 or so and then killing them.

One other shadow I must insert. The number of lunatics in
Ireland in 1901 was four times as great as fifty years earlier, although
the population had fallen by one-third. A doctor at a Dublin
conference put the situation thus : there is one lunatic or idiot in
Ireland for every 178 of the present population and one public
house to every 176.[1] Some of this was attributable to an emigration
which left behind the old and incapable ; some to the return from
the States of emigrants broken in mind and body ; some must be
put down to loneliness and poverty. The average wage of the Irish
labourer at this time (1904), including allowances in kind, was 11/-
per week, but in seven counties it was under 10/-. This compared
with just under 19/- in England, just over 19/- in Scotland, and
17s. 3d. in Wales. There were twelve million acres of pastoral land
to three million of arable. Whole districts had been denuded of
people and given over to bullocks ; labour on the land was isolated
and social life difficult or impossible. Over here we are helped to
keep sane by our proximity to one another.

The Home Rule movement had been launched by Isaac Butt in
1870. Bad harvests in 1879 led Michael Davitt to found the Land
League and in 1880 there were two thousand evictions and in 1881
over four thousand agrarian crimes. The Parnell split took place in
December, 1890, and was patched up with John Redmond as leader
in 1900. In the meantime many Irishmen, surfeited with the
struggle in Westminster and the venomous internecine squabbles of
the Nationalist members, were feeling out for new ways of helping
their country forward. Noble earls and landlords began to confer
together, write pamphlets and speak of devolution. " The broad

---

[1] In 1924 there was one licensed publican for every 250 of the population
of the Free State.

fact " declared the Earl of Dunraven " is that the best in Ireland is flowing outward, the worst is drifting, in increasing proportion, to the lunatic asylums, and the balance remains in Ireland of necessity rather than by choice. It is in the face of these deplorable facts that I appeal to moderate men in Ireland to put aside their differences for a while and do something for the salvation of their country."

Lord Salisbury's twenty years of resolute government (1886-1905) was a see-saw policy of coercion and concession, an amalgam of firmness and appeasement. Rarely has any government of whatever colour passed so many benevolent measures and backed them with more generous subsidies. Gradually despair gave place to a new hopefulness. The first decade of the 20th century saw the birth of the movements which were to make the Ireland of to-day. The story is told of an American visitor to Cork Exhibition, promoted by the Department of Agriculture, observing to Sir Horace Plunkett : " I often saw more things, but I never saw more ideas." It is never easy to read aright the signs of the times, to recognize among the circulating ideas those which are significant, seminal, for the future. I can only plead that I was not more blind than the statesmen of the time in thinking, as did Balfour and Plunkett, that the economic problem was fundamental and would be decisive.[1]

In 1898, Gerald Balfour, one of the ablest and most industrious of Chief Secretaries, had put through Parliament a comprehensive measure of local self-government which replaced grand juries and poor law boards ; it wiped out nominated elements, dethroned the Squires, and substituted 600 county and district councils elected on a parliamentary franchise.

* * * * * * *

[1] Mansergh, *Ireland in the age of Reform and Revolution.* P. 201.

The importance of the land question deserves fuller treatment. The Irish system of tenure differed radically from that of England and Scotland. Over here the landlord provided the more permanent capital outlays, such as house and buildings. The Irish tenants, with absentee landlords, were left to make their own improvements at their own costs. In Ulster the evils of this plan were checked by a custom which had given the tenant a right, a claim on the improvements made. This custom Mr. Gladstone legalised in 1870. It was not intended to create a dual ownership, but in practice it worked out that way. In 1881, after the Land League agitation, the Ulster custom was extended to the whole of Ireland. The tenant was given fixity of tenure, free sale, and a right to have a fair rent fixed by the State. The tenant could not contract himself out of his rights.

Land purchase by the tenant had been envisaged by many statesmen, particularly by John Bright, and provision for this was made in the Acts of 1870, 1885 and 1891. This resulted in two contending policies : purchase, on the one hand, and fair rent-fixing, on the other, and it had become plain to all concerned which was preferable. On one farm the tenant was paying a rent reduced by the Courts, but with no prospect of ownership ; on the next farm, the tenant was paying an annual charge substantially less than the judicial rent and was every day becoming the owner of his land. This was the genesis of Mr. Wyndham's Bill of universal purchase, passed by a Conservative Government in 1903. It set out to abolish landlordism and to create a peasant proprietary. The Gladstonian ideal of dual ownership and fair rents was given up. It was a revolutionary change in the basic industry of the country and in the place of endless agitation it allowed security and stability to take root. With a long-term sinking fund for the tenant and a grant of 12 per cent on the purchase money to the landlord it was impossible to put sales through fast enough.

The predictions then made that Wyndham's stabilizing measure would extinguish the demand for political independence were falsified. Lord Salisbury voiced the prevailing view that a small proprietary afforded the soundest support for the conservative institutions of the country and at the time this view was held by many who assured me that in a few years Ireland would be quiet, prosperous and dull. But observers writing forty years later point out that " the chief legacy of the Land Question was not a peasantry reconciled to ' good government ' but a peasantry who, conscious of their new economic status as owners of land, had been brought once for all into the national struggle ... The solution of the Land Question heralded the emergence of a rural middle class whose control over the Nationalist movement has been challenged frequently but never successfully, a class whose social and poltical philosophy is embodied in the constitution of 1938."[1] This does not mean more than that the fulfilment of Salisbury's prediction has been post-dated, and that " there are things they like better than prosperity."

Another contemporary prediction has been falsified. The spectacle of the revolution afforded by Irish Land Purchase carried through by legislative interference and finance was then thought bound to excite the imagination of the occupiers of land in this country and to presage similar changes. That has not happened. Here the bounty of the State to the farmers has assumed forms more devious and disguised.

A change in land tenure, however revolutionary, left much to be desired. On the one hand, there was the land ; on the other, the man, and as great a revolution was needed in the second as in the first. When I crossed over to Ireland in 1904 there was in County Cavan an enterprising dramatic critic from Fleet Street growing cabbages and speaking his mind with less diplomatic

[1] Mansergh. op. cit. P. 203.

dilution than was common. "The rent of my acre," "Pat," told the world,

> " in the corner of which I grew the cabbages, at the rate of £35 profit, is between 5/- and 6/-. If I were 'a sound Nationalist ' I suppose I'd ignore the £35 and lead an agitation against my landlord for a reduction in the 5/- . . . If you had a man you didn't like on the same ship with you in mid-ocean, would you sink the ship? I would not, but then I'm not 'a leader of the Irish nation at home and abroad.' The Irish nation stands in the position of a man who kills himself in order to kill a person with whom he has had a quarrel. It is hard to say which does the more to destroy the Irish nation—the man that owns the land or the man that occupies it."[1]

I used to like to parallel this passage with one from Sydney Smith :

> " What trash to be bawling in the streets about the Green Island, the Isle of the Ocean ; the bold anthem Erin go bragh. A far better anthem would be Erin go bread and cheese, Erin go cabins that will keep out the rain, Erin go pantaloons without holes in them."[2]

The note of robust economic initiative was now being widely sounded. The man who most clearly proclaimed that you must change the holder of the land as well as the holding was Horace Plunkett. The agrarian agitator put all the emphasis on getting the land from the landlord ; Plunkett on finding a man fit to use the land and make a living by it. He addressed some fifty meetings before he could attract adherents to his gospel. No man worked harder for his country, forgave so much, or was so shamefully rewarded.

[1] *Economics for Irishmen* by Pat.
[2] *Peter Plymley's Posthumous Fragments.*   P. 12.

In 1895 he gathered the more moderate representatives of the clashing creeds into what came to be known as the Recess Committee, of which he was chairman, and it issued a manifesto in favour of a policy of agricultural co-operation.   Banks and creameries followed and a weekly paper—*The Irish Homestead*—edited by a mystical poet, painter, philosopher and rural sociologist, George Russell (A.E.).   In 1899 the Department of Agricultural and Technical Instruction, already mentioned, was set up, and it adopted a technique which was novel at that time in government circles. It did not wait to be asked for advice, it placarded every police station with it : spray your potatoes now ; sow your seed now ; weed your garden now.   It ran a farm and a school of forestry ; it provided stallions, bulls, and boars ; lent money to start hat, hosiery, and fruit factories ; sent out expert instructors from the Royal College of Science ; sent students to London and Germany ; subsidized tobacco growing ; supplied fruit trees and paid half-carriage on all fruit sent to market for the first five years.   Much of this method was modelled on continental, and especially on Danish precedents.   Denmark had left Ireland far behind in the trade in butter, eggs, and bacon, the very goods in which Ireland was potentially qualified to excel.

The co-operative movement and the Department met with bitter opposition from some of the nationalist and unionist leaders and in a triangular parliamentary contest in South Dublin, Plunkett was defeated.

One other movement associated with the policy of killing Home Rule by kindness must be mentioned.   In 1891, Arthur Balfour had founded the Congested Districts Board to deal with the chronic destitution of the West of Ireland.   It was a highly centralised and independent body, bestowing its benefits from above in the absence of any very intelligent demands from below.   Along the seaboard counties from Donegal to Kerry there were thousands of uneconomic holdings which with the available capital and prevailing methods could not keep families in decency and had to be subsidized indirectly by harvest earnings in England and postal orders from America. The Board set itself to enlarge the holdings by the purchase and redistribution of land. During the thirty-two years of its existence (1891-1923) it purchased 951 estates for £9½ millions and spent £2¼ millions on improving the estates before resale to some sixty thousand tenants.

It started supplementary industries : spinning, weaving, lace-making, basket-work. Fishermen were taught to build boats and to catch fish ; boats were sold to them on the instalment system and baptized with the names of Irish saints. These good offices were not always welcomed. When the Board offered to put windows in cabins where looms were being worked by lamplight, only four cabins in a crowded valley would take windows as a gift.

One result of the Balfourian policy was the introduction of carpet making into Donegal by Scotsmen from Ayrshire. Alexander Morton of Darvel was a remarkable handloom weaver, and his son James, the founder of Sundour Fabrics Ltd., even more remarkable. One of them, with expert eyes, had observed a handmade carpet in a London shop or warehouse, and traced it to a convent in Antwerp, where the method of making it was freely explained. At this time, while buying or selling a horse in Belfast, they learnt that the Government was anxious to check emigration from Donegal by finding employment for the native girls. James Morton visited the area and it was not long before four factories were built and five hundred girls employed making the famous hand-tufted Donegal carpets. One of them was specially made for Arthur Balfour's room in 10, Downing Street. Morton often described the first

interview he had engaging the girls, with the local priest as recruit-
ing sergeant, and the unkempt peasant girls coming down to the
village from the outlying country for all the world like droves of
wild hill ponies. By 1906 the ' Donegals' were giving a turnover of
£25,000 a year,[1] and Morton liked to boast that they jumped the
American tariff and adorned the rooms of the President at the White
House. The Mortons were responsible for other innovations which
turned parts of Ireland upside down. They bought land near
Killybegs, introduced a steam plough and grew the best quality
fruit for the rich Glasgow market.

In 1923 the Congested Districts Board was dissolved and its
functions distributed among the Ministries of the Free State.

The best leaders of the country largely succeeded in fixing the
national attention on matters economic, and the amount of space
given to social questions in the Irish press at this time was considerable. The officials of " the Department" frequented meetings
and conferences, took part in discussions, received and replied to
criticism with infinite patience. It was natural to imagine that this
vast and widespread effort to achieve economic salvation by the
union of organised self-help and state-aid would cool political
passions and arrest the separatist movement. As I said above, it
turned out otherwise.

* * * * * * * *

Plunkett published his persuasive and conciliatory *Ireland in
the New Century* in 1904, and simultaneously a little-known
journalist, Arthur Griffith, published *The Resurrection of Hungary.*
and it was in its pages the secret of the future was concealed.
Wherever I went I bought the local newspaper : *The Tyrone Constitution*, *The Derry Sentinel*, *The Sligo Champion* and others
christened with challenging battlecries. They poured out week by

------

[1] Private Memoir by his son, Jocelyn Morton, 1944.

week columns of incendiary invective, bound, you felt, to set the countryside ablaze, but next day you met the harmless editor in the village inn and learnt that he had to earn his living by supplying a commodity which was much in demand. Grievances were endemic and it had become difficult and unpopular to speak with candour on any controversial subject when the blame for every misfortune could so much more easily be put on English mis-rule. Bemuse a people for generations by telling them that but for the English they would be the finest people in the world and they are apt to believe it.

Among the papers I bought was one called *The United Irishman* —there was not much of it and I think it cost a half-penny. It first appeared in 1899, and had been repeatedly seized and suppressed by the police. It was not so much a newspaper as a series of historical and political essays full of information and inspiration. Its standing dish was an exposition of the Hungarian struggle for liberty under the leadership of Kossuth and Deak. In 1904 these articles appeared in a book above the name of Arthur Griffith. It opened with these words :

> " Look at the Map of the World at Hungary. It is a fair and fertile country, inhabited by brave and intelligent people. Sixty years ago it was enslaved, as is Ireland. To-day it stands, a free and prosperous nation, in the front rank of European States . . . Ireland, at the end of the great Artificial Famine, looked not so hopelessly crushed at Hungary at the close of the same year—1849."[1]

It is hard in 1950 to recognize the Hungary which the Irish prophet held up as a model to his countrymen forty years ago. The

---

[1] In Wales the cause of Hungarian nationalism advocated by Kossuth was championed in the *Amserau* (*Times*) by William Rees (Gwilym Hiraethog), preacher, poet and publicist.

Danubian federation of which Kossuth dreamt still seems far off. Now it is Hungary that is crushed and Ireland that is hopeful.

The book closed with an exposition of what was later to become known as the policy of Sinn Fein, and in the Irish Convention, held • in Dublin in November, 1905, Griffith announced himself a disciple of Frederick List, " the real founder of the German Zollverein," the man who had brushed aside the free-trade " fallacies" of Adam Smith and thwarted England's dream of the commercial conquest of the world by laying the foundations of modern Germany.

The core of the Sinn Fein gospel was Irish self-reliance, backed by a moral protection. Given two articles equally cheap and good, buy the one made at home. I recall a conference in Cork where a speaker boasted that he was dressed in seventeen articles of Irish manufacture. Sinn Feiners insisted that where Irish goods were not obtainable at any price, the products of any foreign country should be preferred to those of England, and low-taxed liquor in place of high-taxed liquor. Patriotism took the form of passing resounding resolutions. I made a note of one of them : " That we the committee of the Lisdoonan branch of the United Irish League at this large and representative meeting of farmers, tradesmen and labourers recommend to our people the use of stallions, bulls, boars, etc., which are in the possession of men who love their country and hate obnoxious people, and we call upon all our fellow Nationalists to support such Nationalists." In a gathering of the men of Donegal I noticed that they resolved with enthusiasm that " As men, we shall reject the games of our oppressor."

Griffith opposed the sending of Irishmen to sit in the British Parliament. He revived O'Connell's plan of a Council of Three Hundred which O'Connell had discarded. He urged that the Council should meet in Dublin, discuss and pass measures, and call on the Irish local authorities to enforce them, as though they had originated in the British Parliament.   Kossuth in the forties and Deak in the sixties had used this method against the Austrian Government. Three main duties of the Council would be to protect Irish industries, institute Arbitration Courts, whose decisions would have the binding force of law, and keep Irishmen out of the ranks of the English armed forces.   All this was outlined in 1904 and elaborated in later editions. In 1918 these principles were put into operation.   Little did I imagine in 1904 that seventeen years later I should encounter in 10, Downing Street, their artificer as the chief Irish negotiator and signatory of the *Articles of Agreement for a Treaty between Great Britain and Ireland* or that I should represent the British Prime Minister at his funeral in Dublin, in August, 1922, or that I should then be able from my own knowledge to bear witness to the truth of the words of President Cosgrave at the graveside in Glasnevin : " At no time during his life, during the period that any here knew this man, did he ever say ' Yes' when he meant ' No,' or say ' No' when he meant ' Yes' and when he signed the Treaty with the enemy, whom he had encountered and met and fought during the last thirty years, he meant to keep it.   His signature was his bond for the honour of the nation on whose behalf he had pledged his word." This was on Wednesday the sixteenth.   The brilliant and handsome Michael Collins in the plumage of Commander-in-Chief was a reverent pall-bearer at the funeral.   On the following Tuesday he was shot in ambush, slain by a countryman in his native county. He was a playboy with the performance of a statesman already to his credit, a national hero dead at thirty-two.

A few years before the appearance of the *United Irishman*, the Gaelic League was founded by Douglas Hyde, as a strictly non-political and non-sectarian body whose objects were to maintain and extend the speaking of the Irish language and the study and publication of its ancient and modern literature.   Hyde was the son of a

Protestant clergyman in Connaught ; a medallist four times over
of Trinity College, Dublin, a Divinity student, steeped in European
literature, who could speak, write and dream in Irish. He came in
touch as a boy with old story tellers in Roscommon and Sligo and
collected songs and folk lore. He published Irish texts and translations of what had been handed down by the people for generations.
Hyde's point was that his countrymen were ceasing to be Irish
without becoming English. They were stuck in a half-way house ;
loudly asserting their nationality, while discarding its manners
and customs ; cherishing animosity towards England while imitat-
ing her more and more. The loss of the language meant to many
a starving of the imagination. Hyde directly linked Ireland of the
twentieth century with the Ireland of the seventh ' then the school
of Europe and the torch of learning', and with a romantic past of
dance and song and story. In the West I frequented miniature
eisteddfods, differing from those of Wales in the prominence given
to dancing, especially step or tap dancing with clappers, common
in Rhymney public-houses in my youth.

The task of reviving the language in Ireland was much harder
than in Wales, where it had been preserved by the churches and
preachers and publishers—not by the schools. Spoken Irish survived into the nineteenth century only in remote country districts.
The political leaders, as in Wales, laid no stress on the importance
of its preservation. Daniel O'Connell, who spoke Irish, would have
welcomed its disappearance. It was Thomas Davis, not the
politicians, who insisted that Irishmen should know their native
tongue and their country's history and from this seed, by and by, the
Gaelic League and Sinn Fein were born.

In 1900 the number of schools in which Irish was taught was
about 140,—three years later the number had risen to 1300. With
the coming of the Free State the compulsory use of the language was

widely extended.   In 1926 the number of persons who spoke Irish only was 12,460 out of a total population of just under three millions. Mr. De Valera attributes this situation to England.   " English is a language forced upon the Irish people."   This is a small fraction of the complete truth.   Assume the worst of the English Government, it is fairer to say, as honest Irishmen have said, that if the Irish people themselves had stood by their language as they stood by their faith it would have been impossible for any Government to destroy it.   Here is the verdict of the greatest of all champions of the language, Dr. Douglas Hyde : " What the battle-axe of the Dane, the sword of the Norman, the wile of the Saxon were unable to perform we have accomplished ourselves."   The use of English is a voluntary slavery to a superb mistress.   Who was it forced the galaxy of educated Irishmen from Goldsmith, Swift and Burke to Moore, Shaw and Yeats to woo and cherish the language which is " the greatest medium of expression in the world to-day ?"

Mr. De Valera's policy has been quite clear :

> ' If I were told tomorrow : " You can have a united Ireland if you give up your idea of restoring the national language to be the spoken language of the majority of the people," I would, for myself, say no.'

And he had no illusions : " You have frequently to take the second best.   We have, in regard to certain appointments that have been made, appointments of a technical character, said that where a person has a competent knowledge of Irish, if he is otherwise quali- fied, he has to take precedence over those who may have even better technical knowledge.   If you do not do that, you make no progress."   On which the historian of the Irish Senate, himself an Irish scholar, comments : " This is not progress but retrogression, and it may easily lead to jobbery.   The sacrifices . . . have to be made not by the politicians but by the poor.   If the poor are ill, it is small consolation to them to know that their 'second best' dispensary doctor has 'a competent knowledge of Irish'[1] ... And Mr. O'Sullivan sums up as follows : " The lamentable fact is that whatever politicians may say or think, the vast majority of the people of Ireland care little or nothing about Irish."

The politicial implications of a revival of the language were not stressed by Hyde nor fully realized by Plunkett. Plunkett gave the Gaelic League general support because he saw in it a programme of work for the individual, in contrast with politics which never awakened initiative. He distinguished between nationality and nationalism and did not believe that the League need necessarily be separatist in sentiment.[2] He did not foresee in 1904 that the League was a delayed bomb, that Michael Collins would declare it to be the most important event in the Ireland of the nineteenth century, and that Patrick Pearse would go even further and pronounce it to be the most revolutionary influence that had ever come into Irish history. During the Second World War those who had sought to build an impossible future upon the imaginary past were engaged in moulding the isolated and neutral Gaelic Republic. Hyde was a linguistic not a political revolutionary, who, as often happens, achieved what he did not intend. He wrote : " We hoped that we could keep the nation alive through the language. It never entered my head that it would come to powder and bullets in my time." When the Gaelic League went over to politics, Hyde resigned and went on with his studies. His co-option as Senator (1925) and his election as first President of Ireland (1938) were " the most unpolitical of political appointments."[3]

* * * * * * * *

[1] *The Irish Free State and Its Senate.* By Donal O'Sullivan.   P. 19.
[2] Plunkett : *Ireland in the New Century.* Pp. 150-160.
[3] *Trinity.* Michaelmas 1949. P. 32.

On March, 31, 1908, Augustine Birrell introduced the Irish University Bill to Parliament, declaring that he himself had only accepted the Irish Secretaryship in the hope of being able to deal with the problem. At that time Ireland had two universities, Trinity College and the Royal University, a purely examining body conferring external degrees. In addition there were Queen's Colleges at Cork, Galway and Belfast.

Ten years earlier Haldane, with Balfour's approval, had negotiated privately an agreed plan of university reform with Archbishop Walsh and Cardinal Logue, journeying privately to Dublin and Armagh for the purpose. At Armagh he was received by the Cardinal himself, " scarlet-clad in full canonicals," and after they had talked business, " he opened a door, and there was on the table an enormous dish of oysters flanked by a bottle of champagne" to which we may be sure Haldane was not prevented from doing justice by any Presbyterian scruples.

Balfour put the Haldane plan before the Cabinet where it was thrown out by a small majority. Birrell revived Haldane's scheme in all essentials. He proposed to found two new universities by Royal Charter, one consisting of the Cork and Galway colleges and a new college in Dublin, and the other of Queen's College, Belfast. The Royal University would be dissolved. There would be no religious tests. The governing bodies would be senates and for five years these would be nominated by the Crown. A statutory commission would appoint new professors. Treasury grants would be increased. The bill became law on July 31.

In due course the Belfast University Commission got to work and advertised *inter alia* for Professors of Economics and History. I applied for the Chair in Economics and was placed one of three on a short list. One of the other applicants was so formidable that I was certain he would be appointed and I accepted my fate cheerfully, not to say jauntily, in advance, and was quite at ease in the interview. The chairman was a County Court Judge, James Johnston Shaw, who had been Whately Professor of Political Economy at Trinity College ; he drew up the statutes for Queen's and became Pro-Chancellor. Among the commissioners I recall Sir Samuel Dill, Sir Arthur Rücker and Sir Donald Macalister. There were, I think, one or two others. The dialogue, in essence, was as follows :

Judge : I notice from your papers that this is not your first visit to Ireland. What induced you to come to Ireland ?

Candidate : I had read books about the country and I thought I'd like to meet the people and study their problems at first hand.

Judge : And what, Mr. Jones, is your solution of the Irish problem?

Candidate : I've published nothing, sir.

Judge : Wise man.

Dill : You appear as Barrington Lecturer to have spoken in the north, south, east and west of Ireland. Where did you find the most intelligent audience ?

Candidate : (instantly) In Coleraine, sir.

This elicited a ripple of laughter round the table. Dill had close associations with Coleraine and I knew this.

The formidable rival who on the score of learning ought to have been appointed was a good friend of mine, a native of Omagh, later to be known as Professor W. R. Scott, F.B.A., the occupant of the Adam Smith Chair in Glasgow from 1915 to 1940. He had written a three volume history of the constitution and finance of English, Scottish, and Irish joint stock companies which was on the eve of publication, and he had, unwisely, hurried to each of the commissioners advance copies of the monumental work. It depressed them. At most I had written a sixpenny pamphlet. On this same day, F.M. (later Sir Maurice) Powicke, and Regius Professor at

Oxford, was elected to the chair of History, the other serious candidate being John Lyle Morison, afterwards a professor in the
University of Durham, and mentioned earlier in these pages.

Had I served a seven year apprenticeship in the chair I might
have made a passable Redbrick professor, but I occupied it for one
session only. I enjoyed every hour of my short stay.

I eschewed politics and stuck to economics and education.   Of
the academic staff I found the two teachers of classics the most
attractive, Samuel Dill and R. M. Henry : the former in the words
of Lord Hewart " equally magnificent in form and shy and reserved
in speech" ; the latter a brillliant talker, openly sympathetic with
the Nationalists, and the author of *The Evolution of Sinn Fein.*
The Senator with whom I worked most closely was R. T. Martin, a
solicitor by profession and secretary of the Ulster Unionist Council.
His politics did not interfere with his ardent desire to improve the
quality of the work done at Queen's. He and I were charged to
consider the local demand for the establishment of a faculty of
commerce, and we visited Birmingham together to study the faculty
of which Professor Ashley was then the head.   We drew up a report
in which we recommended against the immediate establishment of
the faculty, but it was set up some years later.   Martin was killed
in a motor accident in 1919 and when years later his wife died, Helen
Waddell wrote a fitting tribute to her in *The Times* :

" Edith Sinclair Martin died on September 23 (1948) in her
seventy-ninth year, one of the remarkable women of her
generation. Born into Victorian ease and convention, she
died Minister Emeritus of a remote congregation in Perth,
pioneer of a movement as yet hardly recognized. For half
her life she was wife to a distinguished lawyer in Belfast, the
mother of children, an admirable political hostess, gay,
arbitrary, and charming to most of the eminent who visited

the city or the university.   In 1915 her only son was killed at
Festubert ; four years later she lost her husband also.   *Hic
incipit vita nova.*   In a life that had lost its meaning she
turned to the discipline of learning, entered Queen's University in her late forties as an undergraduate, and took her
Master's degree in science.   Still unsatisfied, she turned to
theology ; studied Hebrew with an aged Rabbi, took the
degree of B.D., served as assistant in various churches, but
was denied ordination till finally received by the Continuing
Free Church of Scotland and ordained minister of Balbeggie.
There she preached, a dignified ageing Portia, with no
feminine art, but with a massive sincerity and scholarship.
Old age sapped her vitality but not her courage ; in the last
year of her life she was planning a thesis for her doctorate—
the theology of John Cameron, rival to Calvin of Geneva ;
and she had held her fourth grandson in her arms."

In 1600, Belfast had been a fishing village of a hundred cottages,
with a background of forest and bog, but its location at the mouth
of the river Lagan, at the head of Belfast Lough, made certain its
ultimate expansion.   Its accessibility to the coalfields of the Scottish
Lowlands and to cheap overseas transport contributed to its prosperity.   Cotton and flax-spinning mills appeared in the late 18th
century, planted by English and Scottish capitalists who profited
by the recent inventions of Hargreaves, Arkwright and Crompton.
A spacious linen hall was opened in 1785 and already in 1802 a
Belfast Mrs. Tier is writing to her brother, a doctor in Dublin : "You
talk of a Dublin merchant paying a thousand guineas for furnishing
a house.   I heard a Belfast one's wife say she could not fit up her
drawing-room for less."[1]   At this date Belfast was " one of the
most trading towns in the kingdom," with a population of 19,000,

[1] Constantia Maxwell : *Ireland under the Georges.* P. 240.

which by 1851 had risen to 100,000, to 340,000 by the close of the century and it is now around 450,000. Its great development dates from 1847 when the Harbour Commissioners were set up to control the port and 2,500 acres of reclaimed land which provided sites for shipyards and quays, seven miles in length. By 1900, Belfast could boast important shipbuilding and engineering industries and manufacture of linen, tobacco, ropes and twine, whiskey and aerated waters on a large scale. Later came aircraft factories. It was a phenomenal growth, in the course of which sectarianism aligned the population and grouped the Protestants in the Shankill and Sandy Row areas and the Roman Catholics in the Smithfield district and the " Falls," preparing the way for the hostile feuds of later years. After the defeat of the Irish leader, Hugh O'Neill, the six Northern counties were planted with English and Scottish settlers. In the town of Lisburn, eight miles from Belfast, Huguenots had settled after the Revocation of the Edict of Nantes, and helped to localize the linen industry in Ulster. Together with the other Protestants they stamped Belfast with a Calvinistic earnestness ; its industrial leaders were men of exceptional force, whose firms had usually achieved success in the lifetime of one or two supermen. Such was the story of Sir Edward Harland and Lord Pirrie, Frank Workman and Sir George Clark in the shipping world. A big engineering works, exporting machinery to the tea plantations of the Far East, was run by its inventive founder, S. C. Davidson, who had several hundred patents to his credit. Thomas Gallagher, at the tobacco factory, was another self-made captain of industry.

Behind the ports of Belfast and Londonderry spread the 180,000 agricultural holdings of Ulster. Every year, drawn from these tiny farms, there was shipped at these two ports large quantities of bacon, butter and eggs, and hundreds of thousands of store cattle on their way to be fattened for the hungry urban markets across the Channel. The Province was thus full of interest to a student of economics.

Between November and May I lectured at Queen's some sixty times and conducted a dozen ' tutorials' mainly on international trade. The class consisted of twelve men[1] and four women. I made up for my ignorance of technical branches of the subject I professed by inviting local experts to address the students. This I found them most ready to do and they took so much trouble to prepare their lectures that I printed and published some of them. A director of York Street Flax Spinning Company dealt with the linen trade of Ulster,[2] a stockbroker explained the money column of the local newspapers on the day of his visit and so forth. This practice did something to bridge the gulf between the university and the business community. A similar gulf separated the university and the artisans in the shipyards. In this connection I met Thomas Johnston, later to be leader of the Labour Party, and a most highly esteemed Senator in the Irish Free State. There had been a University Extension movement but there was no branch of the W.E.A. in Ulster. Powicke and I took steps to remedy this by stirring up the Co-operative Society and the Trades Council, and by having a tutor appointed to take care of extra-mural work, Russell Jones, a St. Andrews graduate, who in later years was to become Director of Army Education in India.

My days were fully occupied. On one of them our first child and only daughter was born,[3] in itself sufficient excitement for a session.

[1] One of them was Mr. Arnold Marsh author of *Economics for Ourselves, Ireland's New Foundations, Smoke*, etc.

[2] The mill was bombed into ruins in 1941.

[3] Now Mrs. Eirene White, M.P. for East Flint.

" I think I will note dinners, as honest Pepys did " wrote Macaulay. I see from a pocket diary that we dined with Senators and Professors on sixteen occasions, that I lectured seventeen times to business, literary and philanthropic societies, and went ten times to the theatre to see *Merry Wives, John Bull's Other Island, The Showing up of Blanco Posnet, Deirdre, Riders to the Sea* and so forth.

Of the social conditions of Belfast I had learnt much as an investigator of outdoor relief under the Poor Law Commission in 1906. Poor Law practice varied greatly from town to town. Thus in 1905, Belfast Union with a population of 368,000 had on the roll 34 disabled men and 42 women, whereas Dublin with a population of 380,000 had 299 men and 1,094 women ; Derry, population 63,000 had only 6 men and 8 women ; Ballymena 53,000 had 128 men and 369 women.

I had visited many factories, especially those which employed half-timers and out-workers. There was no strong public opinion against these evils. The strain of work in a noisy mill and schooling in ill-ventilated and overcrowded buildings sapped the strength of children as they merged into adolescence, and it was no surprise to find that the death rate of the age group 15 to 20 in Belfast rose to double that of Manchester.

At this time Lord and Lady Aberdeen were at the Vice-Regal Lodge, and Lady Aberdeen did valiant work promoting health measures, especially to counter tuberculosis, by means of lectures and travelling exhibitions. I went to Dublin at her bidding to talk on pauperism and poverty and also on the medical inspection of school children.

Dublin shopkeepers and milliners preferred to have rich spend-thrifts like the Dudleys at the summit and poked fun at the Presbyterian earnestness of Lady Aberdeen. Mr. Birrell was bored with Her Excellency's dinners of divines and doctors and dentists, but with Dublin's record of disease it might have been better for the city had there oftener been more interest in such matters at the top. The Dublin death rate was nearly twice that of London, and nearly half the deaths took place in the various workhouses, hospitals, lunatic asylums and prisons, 43 per cent as against an average of 18 per cent in large English towns.   As in Glasgow, much of the unhealthiness was due to tenement dwellings but also to " graceful Georgian streets" and to densely crowded and degraded Georgian houses. There was no lack of medical officers of health or of inspectors, but in a typical year the penalties inflicted for sanitary offences (including workshops) amounted to £157.   The local administration was obviously at fault.   When later the Free State came into being many local Corporations were suspended for some years.

WALES 1910—1920

A T the end of my first and only session at Queen's we spent our summer holiday with old college friends, Richard and Violet Jones, in Llandinam, a mid-Wales village famous as the birthplace of David Davies, a pioneer of the Welsh coal trade and the founder of a family well-known for its public spirit, its enlightened bene- volence and its patronage of the fine arts.[1] Through the good offices of our host I met the grandson, also David Davies, later, Lord Davies, and his sisters, Miss Gwendoline and Miss Margaret Davies. They were at this time besieged with appeals for letters to sanatoria from consumptives, and these were much in excess of the beds available. We had some talk on the subject, and thus almost casually began a life-long and fruitful friendship.

I had barely returned to Belfast when I was invited to discuss a proposal which the Davies's wished to make to me. They had decided to launch a public voluntary effort to combat the white scourge and they were ready to start it with a gift of £125,000 if I would become the secretary or organizer of the movement.

I had always intended to return to Wales, but there was then no Chair of Economics in being or in prospect in any of the colleges. My wife and I were entirely happy in Belfast and the recipients of every kindness and encouragement. I especially felt deserting R. T. Martin who had been my staunchest helper at Queen's. But this seemed a way back to Wales which would bring me at once up against one of its most widespread social problems. When con- fronted periodically with these fateful domestic crises we wasted

[1] See Ivor Thomas : *Top Sawyer*.

little of our own time or that of our friends in discussion. The
issues were quickly laid bare. An hour or two usually sufficed.
There was always a finger-post at the cross-roads. I accepted the
invitation to return to Wales and gave up the life of a professor for
that of a secretary, organiser, travelling lecturer and beggar. Within
a few weeks I was installed in an office with typists in Newtown, a
few miles from Llandinam, and conveniently placed for my operations to be overlooked by the president of the new organization,
David Davies. A national conference was held at Shrewsbury on
September 30th, 1910, and it launched the King Edward the
Seventh Welsh National Memorial Association and declared its
object to be the eradication of tuberculosis in the Principality.

The goal thus boldly stated has proved wildly utopian, as is
the way with our social ideals, but recent advances in medicine had
been so striking that scientists had boldly declared all epidemic
diseases could be abolished within fifty years, granted the unstinted
application of known methods of inquiry and control. Not only
may ignorance defeat our plans, but the possession of intelligence is
no guarantee of practical achievement. Inertia and selfishness may
be counted on, at all levels of society, to intrude between knowledge
and action. The Welsh people have furnished England and Wales
with many doctors, but they cannot be said to be themselves
seriously troubled or even acutely aware of the high rates of sickness
and death ruling in their midst. There is a large element of fatalism
in their outlook.

Before the national plan of the Llandinam family there had
been earlier attempts to rouse the public to action. In 1903, under
the auspices of the National Association for the Prevention of Consumption, its West Wales branch set out to build the Alltymynydd
Sanatorium (24 beds since increased to 50) at Llanybyther, for the
service of the counties of Carmarthen, Pembroke, and Cardigan.

At the outset Sir John Williams, M.D., whom we met on an earlier page, was chairman, but he had a difference of opinion with the committee and resigned. There followed an acrimonious newspaper controversy (1905-1907) on the value of sanatoria. The ultimate success of the West Wales effort was largely due to P. J. Wheldon, a Carmarthen bank manager. On the foundation of the Welsh National Memorial Association the Sanatorium was presented to it by the Trustees.

The Penhesgyn Open Air Home at Menai Bridge, Anglesey, in grounds comprising some 25 acres, was built and equipped in 1908 by a member of another generous family, Miss A. M. Davies of Treborth, to provide accommodation for 8 young girls. Later it was extended to 16 beds. It is more in the nature of a residential open air school than either a hospital or sanatorium. The child's education goes on alongside the treatment which, being a lengthy process, often extends from eight to twelve months.

In July, 1913, Miss Davies presented the institution to the Association, and for over thirty years she was Chairman of the House Committee.

In 1904 the Denbighshire County Council held a public inquiry in Wrexham into the need for a sanatorium for poor persons suffering from consumption, who could not afford the three to five guineas a week then charged in private institutions. Local doctors testified to the causes of the prevalence of the disease : overcrowding and the spread of infection in damp, cheerless and airless houses ; intermarriage ; apathy and neglect of obvious precautions. Much of the labour of medical men was frustrated by the conditions in which their patients lived. A Chirk doctor gave as a contributory cause the emotional nature of the Welsh, which used up nerve force, a loss that weakened resistance to all diseases.

The position in Wales was sufficiently serious to warrant the

most strenuous efforts to better it.   In the Registrar General's
Report for 1909 "corrected" death-rates for the years 1905-1909
were published for eighteen counties in which the highest mortality
from phthisis ("consumption of the lungs") was recorded.   Ten of
the eighteen counties were Welsh, and in six of them the mortality
was higher than in any English county.   The counties of the English
border—Flint, Radnor, Brecon, and Monmouth—were those with
the lowest mortality, and those on the western littoral had the
highest rates : Anglesey, Caernarvon, Merioneth, Cardigan, Pembroke, and Carmarthen.   The excess affected female much more
than male mortality.   The converse held good in England.

Tuberculosis was only one of the dark pictures presented by the
poor law statistics which reflected the insufficient and ill-cooked
food, the gross over-crowding, the insanitary surroundings, and
the unhealthy personal habits of the population.   In the rural areas
the bulk of the pauperism was due to old age.   In North Wales a
fourth of the women over sixty were drawing out-door relief.   In
urban areas the proportion of pauperism was high at every age and
was connected with accidents and widowhood.   The workhouses,
often over-crowded, were filled with the old, the infirm and the sick,
and there was then little provision for imbeciles and epileptics.   In
the towns hundreds of men, women, and children died "before their
time"   This was specially true of infants.   In the four weeks of
August 1911 there were born in five South Wales towns (Newport,
Cardiff, Swansea, Merthyr and Rhondda) 1,397 infants and 531
died within four weeks, that is a death rate of 380 per 1,000.

The task of the new Association was to awaken the country to
the facts, with special reference to tuberculosis.   This was attempted
by public meetings, lantern lectures, pamphlets, travelling caravans
and exhibitions, and by planning a national scheme of treatment.
We were advised by a small group of medical experts which met in

London. This included Sir William Osler, Christopher (now Lord) Addison who later became Minister of Health, and Dr. Marcus Paterson, who was appointed first Medical Director of the Association, and whose fund of common sense was to prove a valuable asset in sifting the abundant and conflicting advice which reached us. The Advisory Committee proposed a co-ordinated plan of campaign which included :

(a) Education   (b) Machinery of Detection
(c) Treatment   (d) After-care
(e) Research.

Its financial estimates, in the light of later developments, were modest : under (a) well under £5,000 per annum; (b) £10,000 per annum ; (c) annual maintenance cost of sanatoria for 750 beds, £50,000.

There was in these years some controversy as to the value of sanatorium treatment. It arose partly from discharging patients as " cured" in cases when " disease arrested" would have been much nearer the truth. We circulated widely a careful statement signed by Sir Clifford Allbutt, Sir Lauder Brunton, Sir William Osler and Dr. Arthur Latham. They stated roundly that " the majority of existing so-called sanatoriums are inefficient, and the treatment given is not *sanatorium treatment*, but treatment in an institution labelled a sanatorium."

The Advisory Committee sometimes met at the house of Lord (then Waldorf) Astor, 4, St. James's Square, and I began then a friendship which I still enjoy with one of the very best of the men I have known in the public life of this country—able, industrious, modest and most earnestly devoted to the public welfare in many fields. The rich no more than the poor " in the loomp is bad," though they may find it harder to enter the Kingdom of Heaven.

So many references were being made to German experience at this time that I was sent to that country in September, 1911. I went to Berlin, Munich, and Dresden, and visited many institutions. I wrote a report on my return which described the German National Insurance scheme, the treatment of the tubercular in dispensaries, sanatoria, forest camps and open air schools ; the use of tuberculin, German health propaganda, and the organization of the latest Swiss sanatorium. Such are the vagaries of memory— at any rate of mine—that had I not the report before me as I write I should have forgotten this visit almost entirely. I cannot now recall any of the institutions which I examined in great detail, but I see that I stressed the importance of early diagnosis and notification, and I quote an eminent Berlin authority, Professor Keyserling, as telling me : the detection and treatment of contact cases is the strategic point in the fight against tuberculosis.

In Nuremberg on the return journey a young man, bursting with energy, entered our compartment and travelled with us to Ostend, talking all the way. Some years earlier I had met him with R. H. Tawney at a Fabian Summer School in North Wales. He expounded Balkan politics in general and the land system of Galicia in detail. I fell asleep, but my wife listened politely hour after hour to his inexhaustible information. He was bound for Balliol, grew up into one of our leading historians, became an active Zionist and is known as Professor Namier. I now listen to him deferentially at the Athenaeum.

In February, 1911, the Treasury set up a Departmental Committee on Tuberculosis with Waldorf Astor as chairman, and its report (Cd. 6164, 1912) was of much help to us in Wales. Before its publication the National Insurance Act had set up Welsh Insurance Commissioners and they were " to have regard" to the activities of the Memorial Association. " The constitution of the Association" it was stated in the Astor Report, " provides for the representation of every County and County Borough Council, and Insurance Committee in Wales and Monmouthshire." " It has a fund exceeding £200,000 at its disposal" and " has recently taken the necessary steps to obtain a Charter." All that and much besides had been the work of the first twelve months and it was now and for many years to come supported by many public men and women, of whom, among the officers, Lord Kenyon, F. W. Gibbins and (Sir) D. W. Evans were both conspicuous and devoted workers—two qualities not always linked together. It was no easy matter to secure the co-operation of the County and Borough Councils in a voluntary and national scheme of the Memorial type, but it was done and it continued for many years.

" The Welsh National Memorial Association is the only attempt ever made so far towards the establishment, in one special department of human activity, of a body to which the whole of Wales and Monmouthshire stands committed for *executive* purposes and as its sole administrative authority . . . The Central Welsh Board cannot open a school, cannot maintain a school, cannot close a school. Even our National University is mainly and essentially an examining and a degree-conferring body."[1]

Kenyon was for thirty years (1897-1927) a most valuable leader in the public life of Wales. His background was that of a Conservative churchman and landowner. He was a craftsman in wood and metal, a gardener and rode to hounds. He was of splendid stature and presence and without being a scholar had considerable administrative gifts. As Bangor College President and the University's Pro-Chancellor he combined dignity, fairness and firmness in handling the people's representatives and his genial smile and unfailing courtesy made him welcome in any gathering. In the formative period of the University Registry he tried to beguile me into

[1] Sir Percy Watkins : *A Welshman Remembers.* P. III.

accepting a joint post of Secretary *and* Registrar, a mark of confidence which I much appreciated, but felt bound to refuse.

Gibbins was bred a Quaker and as a grown man had such a Spanish visage that he might have stepped out of an El Greco frame. He was a prosperous maker of tinplate in the Neath valley, a County Councillor, a Justice of the Peace, a Treasurer of the National Memorial, and in all offices a man of few but emphatic words, " rampantly honest" Henry Jones called him. For a short period he represented Mid-Glamorgan in Parliament but quickly tired and would have preferred, as he put it, to pay his office boy to walk through the Lobbies. After I settled in London in 1916, we dined periodically at the Great Western Hotel, Paddington, and he kept me in touch with the industrial situation in South Wales as he saw it. He and John Hodge, the men's leader, decided the affairs of the tinplaters privately the night before their official luncheon and business meeting in Swansea and then steered the negotiations publicly to the agreement already reached. Strikes were entirely avoided for many years. Gibbins was willing to pay high wages so long as dividends were kept at a satisfactory level and that meant throughout the period of his management an average of 20% free of income tax. At last after 31 years in the business he decided to sell out in 1921. He put up to J. C. Davies, the managing director of Baldwins, a memorandum running to about six lines. There were 144 shares at a paid up price of £250. Gibbins asked Davies for £1,000 per share making £144,000. After visiting the works, Davies suggested knocking off £10,000. Gibbins agreed and sold each share for £900 odd. Gibbins continued to be a director of the Melin Tin Works in order that he might remain Chairman of the Tinplate Conciliation Board. He died in 1937.

John Hodge, leader of the tinplaters, became the first Minister of Labour. Shortly after his appointment in December, 1916, I was sent to see him by Lloyd-George on some business. The big burly ex-Parkhead puddler was seated at the far end of a spacious and splendid saloon, hung with famous paintings. He greeted me in a booming voice: " Coom in Mister Jonez, 'am sittin' in the drawring-room of the Duke of Buccleuch." At a later interview with a deputation of workers seeking an advance of wages when negotiations were making no progress he turned us Civil Servants out and presently we heard him shouting in very uncivil language: " Not a blasted ha'penny shall you get."

The Memorial Association by means of its network of dispensaries and hospitals and local officers came to possess a far more minute knowledge of the incidence and causes of tuberculosis throughout the Principality than was possible, if imagined, in 1911. Since then the death rate for Wales has fallen from 1506 to 608 per 1,000,000 despite the occurrence of two devastating world-wars. But the figure for England and Wales as a whole is still lower, 458 in 1949. The Association had about 2,000 beds of its own, and rented another 500. The cost of the scheme for the year 1945-1946 was £631,000 and the contributions of Counties and County Boroughs, £548,500. The difference is mainly derived from the contributions of the Ministries of Health and Pensions. In September, 1937, the Minister of Health (Mr. Walter Elliot) set up a Committee of Enquiry into the Anti-Tuberculosis Service in Wales and Monmouthshire and its Report was signed in October, 1938 by Mr. Clement Davies (Chairman) and Dr. Francis Coutts. From 5 July, 1948, the Association passed under the control of the Welsh Regional Hospital Board set up under the National Health Service Act, 1946.

To go back to 1911, there was no difficulty in obtaining the Royal Charter, as we had the support of the Chancellor of the Exchequer. David Davies and I had tea with Mr. Lloyd-George at 11, Downing Street and put our case. This was my first meeting with him. I specially stressed the loss of gifted lives—poets and preachers who had been cut down early by this disease. I reminded him of three well-known young poets, Telynog, Golyddan, and Ben Bowen, who had died at 25, 22, and 25 respectively, and I quoted the familiar verse written by Telynog on the seashore in Cardigan when trying to recover his lost health :

> Blodeuyn bach wyf fi mewn gardd,
>   Yn araf, araf, wywo ;
> A'r blodau eraill oll a chwardd,
>   Tra mi fy hun yn wylo :
> Pan dyr y wawr, bydd perlyn gwlith
>   Ar ben pob un o'r blodau ;
> A minnau'n eithriad yn eu plith
>   Ac etto'n fyw fel hwythau.[1]

These were the words of a song popular in Wales for many years.

This moved the Chancellor and he recalled to us a friend of his in his native village who had died young from the disease. There were hundreds more like him, I interposed, pining away in misery and poverty and scattered throughout Wales. Then suddenly and characteristically he exclaimed : " Why can't I do something for these poor sufferers in my new Insurance Bill which I am now preparing ? It would make an attractive feature." That was the

[1] I am a blossom, and I fade,
  Decay is creeping, creeping ;
All flowers laugh, in joy array'd
  While I am weeping, weeping ;
With pearls of dew, at dawn of day,
  These flowers are adorning,
But meanly garbed among the gay,
  I droop, untrimmed, each morning.
                              M.S.

origin of Sanatorium Benefit. When he introduced his Bill the following passage was part of his speech :

" There are 75,000 deaths a year in Great Britain and Ireland from tuberculosis, and a much more serious fact is that, if you take the ages between 14 and 55 among males, you find that one out of three dies of tuberculosis, and these are the ages which should be those of strength, vigour and service . . . 75,000 deaths a year ! There are 43 counties and towns in Great Britain and Ireland, with a population of 75,000. If one in a single year were devastated by plague, every man, woman and child destroyed there, and the place left desolate —if the same thing happened in a second year, I do not think we should wait a single session. All the resources of the country would be placed at the disposal of science to crush it out."

This legislation directly affected, and at first alarmed, the pioneers of the Association. It was plain that the Welsh Insurance Commissioners would henceforward become our financial masters and policy controllers. A case for special treatment in Wales of its voluntary Association had to be made out and distinguished from the administration of the Act appropriate to England. Gradually, after many conferences, a *modus operandi* was constructed which endured until the other day. I was, meanwhile, being urged in friendly quarters to apply to become one of the Commissioners, and the decision to do what was best for the Association and for myself caused some heart-burning. To quit after only twelve months' work looked like desertion ; on the other hand if I left, the Association would have a friend at court who believed in its policy. Ultimately, it was amicably agreed that I should apply for a post as Commissioner and at the last minute I wrote to the Chancellor offering my services. On January, 1st, 1912, I became Secretary of

the National Health Insurance Commission (Wales) and a Civil
Servant.　I was to remain one till 1930.

My year with the Association had been strenuous.　I journeyed
over Wales to scores of meetings, in an open car, driven by a tubercular chauffeur, who derived much benefit from my treatment of
him.　He had been a student at Aberystwyth and had abused his
throat as a secondary school teacher.　He is not only still alive and
my friend, but he has only just retired from his post as accountant
to an important Scottish firm.　Earlier he had had the sense to
marry a Scottish nurse.

My defects as a lecturer were more than made up for by the
Association's staff of speakers, especially by Dr. R. Owen Morris,
who had been a Mayor of Birkenhead, and by Tom John, who had
been President of the National Union of Teachers.　Dr. Morris was
a born pulpiteer in the two languages and could hold the most miscellaneous audience by his homely illustrations.　Tom John was a
Rhondda product, which means that he was quick, lively and
humorous.　He was short and spherical and at home everywhere
with everybody.　He knew nothing of science and his English and
Welsh pronunciations of *bacillus* and *bacilli* were his own and
variable ; his description of the fight within our bodies between the
white and the red corpuscles (also a word of uncertain sound) resembled that of a match between Jimmy Wilde and Freddie Welsh ;
it provided some instruction and much entertainment.　For reliable
statistics I could always count on J. E. Tomley of Montgomery, an
indefatigable supporter of the Association.

David Davies was thirty when he and his sisters founded the
Memorial Association.　He was its President and was already
displaying the creative and bold and unselfish qualities which were
to prove so influential for the next thirty years of his strenuous life.
He had then boundless, untamed energy and released much of it in

the hunting field chasing the fox or the otter. He would ride up at nine or ten o'clock in the morning to the office door in Newtown on his way to a meet, arrayed in the kit of a M.F.H., and issue, rapidly, enough detailed instructions from his fertile mind to occupy the small staff a month executing them. He would call back in the late afternoon expecting to find them all carried out A fraction of them were, but he had no experience of the time taken up by detailed administration : he had always given orders and naturally was impatient of contradiction, of delay or resistance to his plans. Most very rich young men suffer from a similar defective training. Twelve months at a desk, or in a coalpit in his youth would have taught him to work with others. Usually his instructions were sound and sometimes strikingly original, but public officials and councillors and professional men, doctors for example, have sometimes to be argued with and gently persuaded to courses of action for which no precedent can be quoted. The President took some managing and that is what secretaries are for. Only a man with David Davies' known generous impulses, disinterestedness and driving force could have overcome, as he did, the obstacles in the way of the Association, and placed it on a firm foundation.

My chief and important contribution to the Insurance Commission was to select (Sir) Percy Watkins to be Deputy Secretary and to enrich its young staff with promotable recruits. I recall Howell E. James who became Chief General Inspector of the Ministry of Health ; Dr. D. J. Roberts, Regional Director for Wales of the Ministry of Works ; and Sir Frederick John Alban who succeeded Sir D. W. Evans as secretary of the Welsh National Memorial Association, and has since become Chairman of the Welsh Regional Board of the Ministry of Health. James Evans, to whom I have referred on an earlier page as my Tredegar friend, was an older generation, and he became Chief Poor Law Inspector in Wales. The

Commission's Accountant, J. C. Morgan, was an experienced Civil Servant, and he taught me how to submit myself in the correct terminology when approaching their Lordships of the Treasury. Dr. D. Llewelyn Williams was the faithful and patriotic Deputy Medical Officer who had served with Welsh troops in France,

I can also claim to have done something to prevent (Sir) John Rowland (1877-1941) running the Commission in his own, to my mind, undesirable way. Rowland was a Cardiff school-teacher who had become one of Lloyd-George's Private Secretaries, first at the Board of Trade and then in Downing Street, and had especially looked after his chief's Welsh interests. He was now one of the four Insurance Commissioners, and there was little he had not learnt in Whitehall of the ways of the Press and of Parliament. He was an ardent and watchful Welsh patriot, a zealous champion of the rights of the Principality, and an advocate of administrative autonomy. He was deeply and darkly ambitious with a determined if tortuous love of power united to ability, industry and exceptional shrewdness. In his presence I felt surrounded by an invisible web. He had an enigmatic smile, ears that could hear the grass grow, and he used to boast of a black deed box in which he had stored letters, or copies of letters, or other explosive material. The violence of his anger so compressed his lips and abbreviated his speech that the few words which escaped from him on such outbursts were incomprehensible either as English or Welsh. He seemed to take pleasure in the literal enforcement of regulations and in officious interference if they were transgressed in the letter. Our relations became correct rather than cordial. I am reminded of the relations of Sir Henry Robinson and Sir Matthew Nathan in Dublin Castle. According to Robinson, Nathan "had rather an embarrassing way, after he had had an interview with any official, of committing to writing a full statement of his recollection of everything that had passed and at subsequent interviews this statement would be produced from a pigeon-hole and used to refute some point under discussion. His written statements were often so surprising that I also used invariably to put down my recollection of what had transpired, so as to be ready for him if he produced any embarrassing paraphrase of our conversations."[1] Rowland rightly stressed the importance of the Commission issuing its circulars and regulations in Welsh, but official terminology was then in its infancy and a specialist had to be engaged for the task of translation. Even so, we laid ourselves open to criticism and the renderings of technical terms were probably unintelligible to the great majority of readers of Welsh.

This division at the top between a member of the Board and its Secretary was apt to infect the staff below and it was just as well that I was transferred to London in December 1916. In 1919, the Commission became the Welsh Board of Health and the potent influence of Lloyd-George, it was said, brought Rowland the chairmanship of the Board in 1930. He was knighted in 1938 and retired in 1939. Other and more profitable activities of the Board have been recounted by Sir Percy Watkins and I need not repeat the story here.[2]

Watkins was a man of very different qualities from Rowland. He was born in 1871 at Llanfyllin, Montgomeryshire, and perhaps the happiest day of his life was that on which he was given the freedom of this ancient borough—a gift rarely bestowed. He died in May, 1946.

His life was that of an administrator—a life learnt in no school or college, for which he underwent no technical or professional training. He was never a student at a university college ; he never graduated except as the recipient of an honorary degree of the

[1] *Memories : Wise and Otherwise.* P. 223.
[2] *A Welshman Remembers.* Chap. V.

University of Wales. It is true he was for five terms at the well-known Grammar School at Oswestry. That was all the strictly academic preparation he had for a life which was to be spent with scholars and colleges, with Boards of Health and Boards of Education.

An administrator is a person who knows the rules which govern the institution whose servant he is. He understands Acts of Parliament, Orders in Council, Clauses and Regulations, when they apply and when they do not ; he can guide a gathering through the mazes of debate, draft a resolution or frame an amendment, as required by the sense of the meeting. But he must know not only the law but the prophets : the professors and laymen, the aldermen and councillors, the ministers and civil servants ; know how they behave in court or council or committee. All this was meat and drink to Sir Percy. He delighted in conferences and knew how to crystallise a discussion at the right moment into an agreed formula. These gifts carried him to Whitehall where they raised the national reputation several points.

His disposition was positive and constructive within conventional limits. He was neither aggressive nor was he obsequious. Normally he was unhurried and unworried. He wanted things done, but he was an open and frank, not a devious and dark conspirator ; he was transparent. Like most of us he liked his own way best, and he could, especially as he grew older, be obstinate, if he did not get it. But after the most fractious debate he bore no rancour. The amount of unselfish work he did for Wales is incalculable—for the University, for the Council of Music, for the Council of Social Service, for the South Wales Settlements, for Coleg Harlech, for the W.E.A. He had no party politics nor close Church attachments that I ever discovered, and I knew him well. He watched football and cricket matches, loved a good story and told many. A few

years ago he published " A Welshman Remembers." In its entire
naturalness the book is an exact mirror of its author, a man whose
tender, generous heart sometimes ran away with his judgment ;
sentimental and almost naive in places, but in the grain it is a book
of a man endlessly kind and staunch and true.

My relations with Rowland were exceptional. I do not dislike
actively nor make enemies easily. I have never deliberately dreamt
of enlarging the realm of hate as, according to Yeats, some Irishmen
have done and a few Welshmen are now doing. It was John
O'Leary who wrote : " There are things a man must not do to save
a nation." I did, it is true, have a strained period with Lord Davies
because I opposed the uprooting and removal of his secretary, Major
Burdon Evans, to England from Newtown, and succeeded in retain-
ing his valuable services for Montgomeryshire. I cannot recall any
other even temporary estrangement in a long life.

I turn to a pleasanter topic. Sometime in 1912, David Davies
had invited an old school friend and artist to Plasdinam to paint his
hunters and hounds, Murray Urquhart. I spent an evening with
them and naturally the talk turned to the remarkable collection of
pictures on the walls which Urquhart now saw for the first time. The
ladies had left the dining-room and Urquhart was regretting that
the collection of pictures was unknown and unseen by the world at
large. " I remember so well," he writes to me, " that you im-
mediately left the room to put the matter before the two sisters.
I don't think it was more than ten minutes or a quarter of an hour
before you came back saying that the idea was approved of."

The Exhibition was held in February and March, 1913, the first
under the auspices of the National Museum, Cardiff, of which Dr.
Evans Hoyle was then Director and Lord Mostyn President. It
drew some thirty thousand persons to see it. The illustrated
catalogue lies before me. There were four Corots, and five Millets,

including the monumental 'Une famille de paysans' and 'Les étoiles filantes'—the story of the luckless Paolo and Francesca, doomed eternally to traverse space together. This had only just been purchased at the famous Rouart sale in Paris. There were Turners, Whistlers, and a landscape by Richard Wilson. In the course of the exhibition lectures were delivered by Laurence Housman, D. S. McColl, Patrick Geddes, Frederick Wedmore, Urquhart, and Hugh Blaker. It was Hugh Blaker who had been the chief adviser of the Misses Davies in making their collection. He himself was an artist and poet and curator of the Art Museum at Bath. At his death, *The Times* (7 October, 1936) wrote of him : " His power of discerning the hand of the great masters was born not only of vast knowledge and experience but even more of a deep passion for the great and fine in art. He was among the first in this country to acclaim Cezanne as a master." His first important discovery was an unrecognized portrait by Rubens which he picked up in the sale-room for some £60. He sold it for around £5,000 to the Kaiser Frederick Museum in Berlin and received the cheque for it a day or two before the outbreak of the first World War. His most remarkable discovery was the large Velasquez of St. John Baptist. This he brought at Christie's for eighty guineas, all the experts jeering. He established it as an authentic work of the young Velasquez and sold a half share to a leading art firm for, it was said, £4,000, and then it went to one of the American galleries for £12,000.

* * * * * * *

While the Memorial Office was at Newtown we had moved our home to Llandrindod for the year I was with the Association. We now moved once more, to Barry where we had a house overlooking the Bristol Channel and in it a large attic, known as the Crow's Nest, where at week-ends I edited, really if not nominally, the first three volumes of a monthly illustrated magazine called *The Welsh*

Outlook, in the founding of which I had had a finger, or perhaps a hand. For one or two winters I also ran a W.E.A. class. In Barry at that time lived several Welshmen who, while not exactly forming a group, saw much of one another: Edgar and Gwen Jones, Silyn and Mary Roberts, Annie Ffoulkes and R. Williams Parry. Edgar Jones was perhaps the most popular of the secondary schoolmasters of his day and has survived to enjoy many civic and national honours. His " boys " are planted in all sorts of key positions at home and abroad, for he is much more than the conventional headmaster. In Cardiff there were kindred spirits, among them Percy Watkins and W. J. Williams, who were to become respectively Permanent Secretary, and Chief Inspector of the Welsh Department of the Board of Education. All had much to do with the *Outlook* and other literary adventures and all have done much for Wales.

It was a period of comparative national prosperity. In 1913 the output of coal was at its peak. Contributions to industrial assurance companies, collecting societies and savings banks were mounting by many millions per annum. We wanted to translate this wealth into a higher quality of social life in Wales. The first effect of the failure of public opinion to keep pace with the spate of Lloyd-Georgian legislation was to increase the number and power of civil servants, and the Labour Movement tended to enthrone groups of county councillors who wielded large patronage in local, which often meant sectarian appointments. Our first notion had been to found a weekly paper in which to expound and criticize the changes afoot. Two previous attempts had failed : the *Welsh Weekly* published for a few months in 1892 and the *Welsh Leader* which lasted from 1904 to 1907. The Monthly *Wales* was a casualty of the War.

Wales was at this time more than ever a seething cauldron of unrest and conflict and this was the theme of the *Foreword* I wrote for our new monthly. The older generation clung to Liberalism, but in the coalfield the young were turning to Socialism and to Syndicalism. From 1875 and through the eighties and nineties Sliding Scales had regulated wages in accordance with the selling price of coal. This method was displaced in 1898 after much strife between masters and men and the South Wales coalfield was then linked with the Miners Federation of Great Britain who fixed wages by negotiation. The protagonist of the change was William Brace, a young Monmouthshire miner employed in the Abercarn collieries. The Secretary of the new South Wales organization was Tom Richards, the first of the Welsh miners' representatives in Parliament to announce his allegiance to the Labour group, soon to be affiliated to the new Labour Party. William Abraham (Mabon) had been elected to Parliament in 1885 and was to remain there after seven successive elections for over a quarter of a century. He was a Liberal and Smillie has described the secret of his leadership :

> " If any friction arose and pandemonium threatened . . . he promptly struck up a Welsh hymn or . . . " Land of my Fathers." Hardly had he reached the second line, when with uplifted arms, as though drawing the whole multitude into the circle of his influence, he had the vast audience dropping into their respective " parts," and accompanying him like a great trained choir. It was wonderful, almost magical and the effect was thrilling. When the hymn or song was finished he raised a hand, and instantly perfect silence fell. The storm had passed."[1]

It should be added that Mabon possessed a physical presence of large and commanding proportions from which issued his melodious voice. He and Richards were Welsh-speaking.

[1] Robert Smillie : *My Life for Labour.* P. 62.

The coalfield continued through the first quarter of the new century to be the cockpit of many battles, in the course of which it threw up a succession of notable leaders : Mabon, Tom Richards, William Brace, Vernon Hartshorn, A. J. Cook and Frank Hodges became national figures known throughout Great Britain. They had all worked as boys in the mine, were products of Sunday Schools, local preachers, more deeply steeped in the Christian doctrine of the value of human personality than in any economic theory. They had been taught that man was not mere means but an end in himself and greater than miner or coalowner or nation or Sovereign State.

These leaders dealt with an inflammable population easily ignited by what they felt to be injustice, and although tamed and civilized by religion and tradition, and upheld and guarded in decent behaviour by social props and fences, primitive barbaric instincts were never far below the surface and these could most easily be released by an excess of alcohol. Wild orgies of violence sometimes disfigured the hymn-singing valleys as in a recent outburst only two or three years earlier than the time of which I am writing. The police had proved unable to control the mob, the Riot Act was read, the troops fired and killed several in the crowd and wounded others. Strikers and sympathisers for miles around gathered to avenge their comrades and maddened with drink proceeded to create pandemonium. That was in the Llanelly area in August 1911.

In North Wales the social structure was better balanced between agriculture, industry and well-to-do visitors from Liverpool, Manchester and the Midlands. Everyone enjoyed more elbow-room. It had rarely been necessary to order troops into the area to quell or shoot a turbulent mob.[1]

In the colleges and in the Welsh quarterly, *Y Beirniad*, John Morris Jones was creating a new school of literature and criticism. The opposition of the chapels to the drama had almost disappeared

[1] See David Williams : *Modern Wales*. P. 233.

and nonconformist ministers were writing plays and rehearsing players. At Aberystwyth, J. O. Francis had written *Change*, and D. T. Davies *Ble Ma Fe* (Where is he ?) and both had been produced by Old Students. Early in this same year, 1913, Cardiff students had produced W. J. Gruffydd's satirical comedy *Beddau'r Prophwydi* (The Graves of the Prophets).

The promoters of the *Welsh Outlook* held their first Board meeting in Cardiff on 25 October, 1913, and resolved on its name. " The Red Dragon " was rejected. We were soon to be told that we should have called it " The Cosmopolitan Outlook," because we " loved some things more than the land of our birth." We had little technical knowledge of how to produce or market the journal, but we found a firm of good Cardiff printers then directed by an optimist and a Barry neighbour, Frank Murrell. He readily responded to our insistence on a standard of printing and illustration hitherto unattained in Welsh periodicals. Margaret Lindsay Williams designed a poster with ornament derived from the Irish Book of Kells. The finance was guaranteed by David Davies who was represented on the editorial board by its chairman, W. J. Burdon Evans. The first number appeared in January, 1914.

Criticism was soon mingled with praise. The chairman complained that in an article on the Civil Service we had supported equal pay for men and women. Our patron thought we gave too much space to music and art. " There is still a lack of profound criticism and of something with a sting in it." " Can't you get someone like Belloc to write a review of the military operations each month ? " Bachelors of Music were disappointed at our failure to notice their immortal compositions.

The journal during its twenty years (1913-1933) underwent many vicissitudes in the course of a succession of editors. Amongst them I recall E. H. Jones, author of *The Road to Endor*, T. Huws

Davies and Edgar Chappell. Huws Davies was a product of the same area, school and college as Sir John Rowland but a complete contrast in character and gifts. He was a generous and mercurial spirit, sociable and enthusiastic, whose breathless flashing eloquence on public occasions in both languages I have rarely heard equalled. For the exuberant inspired moment he was completely sincere and convincing, a romantic, over-orchestrated Celt. It was to his friends amazing that with such an effervescent temperament at the same time he did so well as secretary of the Welsh Church Commission : his blend of good nature, real ability and popularity with all classes in the Principality, irrespective of political and religious opinions, carried him through triumphantly.

The average net sale of the *Outlook* in its first nine months was 3,113 copies per month. Then came the War, but we held on and even embarked on publishing plays, poetry and fairy tales, usually in Welsh, which were subsidized by three Liverpool Welshmen who deserve honourable mention : Sir R. J. Thomas, W. O. Roberts and J. Evan Morris. Mr. Morris joined later in publishing *Byd y Blodau* (1924) and an English edition *Flowers of the Wayside and Meadow* (1927). Mrs. Silyn Roberts when visiting Denmark had noticed a book in use in the schools containing some beautiful coloured illustrations of flowers, which were, in the main, indigenous to both Denmark and Wales. Permission was obtained from Professor Lange of the Smallholders College, Odense, to use his original illustrations and Professor Lloyd Williams of Aberystwyth was induced to provide a Welsh text. To extract this text from its author took much pressure and patience but it arrived at last. Messrs. William Lewis produced both versions, and copies were widely distributed among the schools of Wales.

Even with subsidies from shipowners and provision dealers we were able to reward our Welsh authors most inadequately. Miss

Annie Ffoulkes edited an anthology of Welsh poetry, *Telyn y Dydd*.
Poets were surprised to be paid at all. ' Goreu tâl, tâl heb ei ddis-
gwyl.'[1] wrote W. J. Gruffydd. " Nid oeddwn yn disgwyl dim,'
wrote Gwynn Jones ' a buaswn yn fodlon i'r swm fynd at drysorfa
i gyhoeddi rhagor o lyfrau Cymraeg.'[2]

When and where Silyn Roberts and I first met I cannot now
remember ; we were fast friends thereafter. I was a year his senior;
he came from the quarries of the North and I from the coalpits of
the South. He found his way to Bangor University College and
advanced further in a ministerial career than I did, having charge
of a church in Lewisham, London, and in Tanygrisiau, Merioneth.
Interesting is perhaps the word which best describes him as a
preacher ; he spoke quietly and from his opening words seized the
attention of his congregation by virtue of uniqueness in choice of
word, imagery and train of thought. Young people were particularly attracted, especially by his frequent presentation of Christ's
personality, as a young man himself who would have understood
their problems. But Silyn did not rest content with a pulpit. In
his youth he was a poet, in love with beauty in all its forms. A
volume of lyrics which he published jointly with W. J. Gruffydd had
an emancipating influence on native convention, liberating it from
moralising, didactic thraldom both in the realm of language and of
ideas. Some two years later he published his Crown poem in
" Trystan ac Esyllt a Chaniadau Eraill " and this was his last volume
of poems. He turned to prose and wrote a few short stories in
Welsh which appeared serially in a Ffestiniog weekly and he translated from Maupassant and other French writers into Welsh.
France had a fascination for him and Paris was a magical city to

---

[1] " The best pay, the pay unexpected."
[2] " I expected nothing and would have been willing that the sum should
   go towards publishing more Welsh books."

which his mind turned with yearning when surfeited with Calvinistic theology.   I often wondered how his career would have shaped had he gone there straight from the college at Bangor.   Would he have worked his way into the Sorbonne associating himself with a group of enthusiasts in international affairs and becoming a leader ?   He possessed qualities which quickly won him friendship abroad : his bonhomie, his sense of humour and subtle awareness of humour in others wherever he met it, his earnestness and capacity of absorbing himself completely in matters of the moment.   Later on, however, he did visit several of the countries of the Continent and he spent five months in America, going as far as Los Angeles.

Instead of developing into a man of letters in which he might have added to the distinction he had so early achieved, he became in 1912, at the age of 41, the Secretary of the Appointments Board for Wales and spent the next six years fitting Welsh graduates into jobs.   During the War he also acted as Secretary in Wales of the Inns of Courts Officers' Training Corps, dealing with some 1500 applications for Commissions.   His next post was stranger still. In 1919 he was appointed Director of Industrial Training under the Ministry of Labour.   There were several thousand disabled men waiting for training and Silyn took an old woollen mill in Newtown and a disused aircraft factory at Cardiff and converted them into instructional factories.   In these and half-a-dozen smaller centres spread over Wales a score of trades were taught : plumbing and plastering, tailoring and bootmaking, hair-dressing, French polishing and so forth.   He astonished his friends with his gifts of organisation and they supported him when in 1921 he applied for the post of Registrar to the University of Wales.   He was rejected and then found congenial work promoting Adult Education in North Wales.   With driving energy he organised W.E.A. classes throughout the counties, going into every hole and corner of remote

places in all sorts of weather.   There was a quick response to his
eagerness and ardour ; the young people seemed only to be waiting
for his call and he could coax the right type of man to become a
lecturer.   He himself joined their ranks and held classes in his own
inimitable way right up to his death in 1930.   The organisation of
classes was continued for fifteen years with notable success by his
widow.   Silyn had through all his public life been deeply attached
to the Labour Movement and had great hopes of the Russian
Revolution.   He spent a month in Russia in the summer of 1930,
caught a fatal germ—rumour said typhus—and returned to die at
home in the early part of his sixtieth year.

The early death of no friend have I regretted more.   We talked
much together : he knew so much more poetry than I did and could
recite one splendid passage after another for miles on our walks,—
Keats, Shelley, Swinburne, Gwynn Jones.   He was, too, an inimitable story-teller.   Had he deliberately starved this side of his
nature in order to help his countrymen to bread and butter and to
the blessings which accompany study?   Williams-Parry's remarkable poem composed soon after Silyn's death somewhat supports
this suggestion.   In this poem the poet stands at his friend's grave
and exhorts him to rise : " Silyn, the Sasiwn approaches, the
'Steddfod week is not far off, an educational conference will soon be
meeting."   There is not much stir in the grave until the poet laments
the perishing of young workmen's talents because the master is no
longer there.   And the tomb can now no longer hold its captive.

> Yna anadlwn drwy y glyn
> Neges gyffrous y geiriau hyn :—
>   " Yn Llanymynydd y mae gwanc
>   Addysg ar ddeunaw disglair lanc."

" Eu doniau'r awrhon sydd dan rwd
Heb obaith cymorth athro brwd."
Ni byddai graig na dorau dwys
A gadwai Silyn dan y gŵys.

I am sometimes led to think that Silyn was indeed meant for Adult Education work, but at other times I wonder if we, his countrymen, failed to find the right job for him who had found the right job for so many others ! What I do know is that I loved the man and that I admired his handling of all his tasks.

*   *   *   *   *

The *Outlook* was hardly safely launched on its career when in the autumn we were overtaken by the outbreak of War. I found an additional interest as Secretary of the Committee which looked after Belgian refugees arriving in Wales. On August 2, 1914, the German Government sent an ultimatum to Belgium demanding passage through Belgian territory. Two days later German troops crossed the Belgian frontier and attacked Liège. Then followed in quick succession the capture of Namur, Brussels and Mons. On October 9th Antwerp fell, and on the 14th, the Germans secured their control of Belgium by seizing Ostend.

The spectacle of a small and peaceful country seized by the throat by a treacherous bully nowhere stirred deeper sympathy than in Wales, and admiration for Belgian resistance knew no bounds. When the refugees began to pour into Folkestone and London, the Lord Mayor of Cardiff (Dr. James Robinson) was quick to form a local refugee committee, and on September 7th the first contingent of refugees arrived in the Principality. The Roman Catholic Bishop offered a school as receiving depot, the Salvation Army provided a " Metropole " as a shelter for women and children, the Plasnewydd Presbyterian Church set an example which was widely followed of renting and furnishing a private house for the maintenance of a Belgian family. Neighbouring towns began to demand their quotas and Cardiff became a distributing centre for South Wales.

The refugees were collected in the London depots and hurriedly conveyed to Paddington by the score. They had only the vaguest notion of their destination, and there was no time for explanations. Their places were urgently needed for fresh arrivals. In the train their names and ages and occupations were jotted down. On reaching Cardiff, they were amazed to find the streets lined with thousands gathered to give them a delirious welcome. Mounted soldiers and police protected them from the caresses of the thronging crowds. The Grand Hotel was packed with excited women demanding " a brave little Belgian." The puzzled Belgians themselves sat around the hall, silent and submissive, gripping their miserable bundles, and then found themselves jerked away in a motor-car.

Those early days were days of universal sympathy and good-will. There were as yet no wounded soldiers of our own. The pent-up emotions of the people flowed freely towards the newcomers. Some idea of the speed with which help was forthcoming may be given by the following incident :

On a Monday afternoon, in October, Professor Waxweiler, of the Sociological Institute, Brussels, telephoned to a friend in Cardiff, begging for clothing for the use of wounded soldiers who were being sent from Antwerp to the neighbourhood of Ostend. On Wednesday morning 30,000 articles of clothing were landed on the quay at Ostend from Cardiff. This achievement was mainly due to the Hon. Violet Douglas Pennant, then a member of the Welsh Insurance Commission.

There were not at first enough Belgian refugees to go round. Many orphan children would have been adopted had they been available, but the refugees came in batches, with mothers-in-law, brothers-in-law, uncles and cousins. Problems of employment, of prohibited areas, of differences of manners and appetites, had not been envisaged. No one thought the War would last long. What more natural than that the refugees should set about making articles which they would need on their return home. But they were not all cabinet-makers. Some were fishermen—but their wives were in a frightened and bewildered state, and would not let them go to sea. Most wanted clerical work. Some refugees thought that Cardiff was El Dorado, and that the British Government's offer of hospitality absolved all Belgians from the necessity of work for the period of the War. On the other hand, the trade unions were apprehensive lest Belgians should displace British workmen. No single solution was possible. As many methods as there were individuals were tried. Boys and girls were sent to school and quickly learnt English. A few learnt to speak Welsh. Domestic service absorbed some young women, and others rewarded their hostesses with fine needlework. About a fifth of the refugees were men, and they remained the chief difficulty. As the War wore on the question why they were not serving at the front was asked with louder insistence, and it became less easy than at first to say that it was not possible for the Belgian Government to arm and equip them.

Mingled with the rank and file, representative of " the bizarre melange of racial, linguistic and religious antinomies " characteristic of Belgium, were a number of distinguished refugees, for whom the Llandinam family had undertaken a special responsibility. At the suggestion of the Misses Davies, Major Burdon-Evans and I crossed the channel to collect and bring to Wales Belgian poets, painters, sculptors, musicians and politicians, who were on holiday along the coast between Ostend and the Dutch border when the war broke out.

It so happened that I knew a student at Aberystwyth, Elsie Dugard, who was engaged to be married to a Belgian "intellectual." We found M. Poldermann at Bruges and enlisted his co-operation in our unusual errand.   We penetrated as far as Ghent, where we saw a wounded German soldier brought in as a prisoner to the Town Hall, and there we met M. de Weert, the first hostage to be selected when the German General von Beseler entered the city.   In a few days we collected over a hundred men and women who were glad to cross with us to England on the last boat but one to leave Ostend, before the arrival of the enemy.   We rested overnight at the Gwalia Hotel in London, and then distributed the mixed assortment in various homes in Wales.   Georges Minne, a sculptor, and a numerous family, settled at Llanidloes ; Valerius de Sadelier, " with the eyes of a primitive," went to Aberystwyth, where he painted winter scenes, almost in monochrome.   And so forth.

On one memorable week-end we gathered at our house in Barry, three of the most famous Belgians, who talked and smoked endlessly; Emile Claus, a painter of Flemish landscapes bathed in sunshine ; Emile Verhaeren, the poet of the Little Towns of Flanders, and Emile Vandervelde, the Belgian Socialist leader and Foreign Minister, after Jaurès and Briand, " probably the greatest orator employing the French language in his day." Madame Claus and Madame Verhaeren were also with us and P. Mansel Jones, now Professor of French at Bangor, then engaged in a study of Verhaeren, which he published in 1926. Of our foreign guests, I found the poet the most attractive. Compared with the politician and the painter, he was shy, gentle and modest, however strong and stormy his poems— ' barbaric' they were sometimes called.   He and his wife were considerate of others, and we were put to various wiles to help them by arranging, for example, that he should be invited to lecture at the colleges and elsewhere at what we persuaded him were normal fees,

but which were really personal to him. Though he was, with
Maeterlinck, at or near the summit of European letters and his fame
established all over the continent, he was not known in this monoglot
country. Miss Horniman's Company had performed his tragedy
The Cloister in Manchester in 1910. The *New Statesman* did something to remedy matters by publishing his poem *La Cathedrale de
Reims*, and an appreciation of his work by Remy de Gourmont, and
Le Cloître was given in French at the Kingsway Theatre in London,
in January, 1915. *The Manchester Guardian* published in French
(with an English translation), his impressions of a visit to Manchester. This included a highly appreciative reference to Richard
Wilson, the Welsh artist's landscapes in the city's Art Gallery.

> " Not far away I notice some Wilsons. The place of this
> painter in English art seems to be very significant. Just as
> Turner did, he understood the classical atmosphere of land-
> scape. Claude Lorraine was his teacher, but for all that he
> could put a human figure in full sunlight better than the
> great French painter could. At the Leeds Gallery one of
> his pictures, called *Landscape with Boys*, overcomes this
> simple but great difficulty most happily and with perfect
> ease."

A Belgian artist who found asylum in Cardiff was Emil Fabry, a
mural painter, who had decorated civic buildings in Brussels and
Milan, or was it Turin ? He wished to express his gratitude for
Welsh hospitality and I suggested a panel to adorn the entrance
hall of the University College. The theme was agreed with Principal
Griffiths and Herbert Thompson, the College Treasurer. It was to
illustrate the Seven Ages of Man, and the central figure turned out
to be a magnificent male nude bestriding a magnificent horse. When
the Principal saw the preliminary sketch he blurted out, " But this
is a mixed college, what will the parents say ?" And the artist,

when he grasped what was meant, replied hopelessly, " Of course I can put trousers on him." How far Fabry proceeded with the painting of the panel I have forgotten ; I do not think it was exhibited, if it ever survived the Principal's *douche*.

When war broke out there were many works by Belgian artists on view in Venice, Florence and Lyons, and in Edinburgh, Glasgow, and Aberdeen. These were gathered to Cardiff under the aegis of the National Museum in the spring of 1915, and we were able to see their paintings of collieries and furnaces, miners and puddlers, our own familiar Welsh surroundings, as well as landscapes and peasants, handled unfamiliarly as subjects of art. Some eyes were opened for the first time.

From 1914 onwards for some years I was much involved with David Davies, Dr. Meredith Richards, the medical member of the Insurance Commission, Sir Ewen Maclean and others in an attempt to guide the generosity of Sir William James Thomas, a South Wales coalowner, in his desire to expand the Medical School attached to the University College at Cardiff. The School had been opened away back in 1893 and provided tuition for the first three years of medical study. It owed its origin largely to a local doctor, W. T. Edwards, and its development largely to the Dean of the Medical Faculty, Professor David Hepburn. The offer of Sir William James Thomas was of the order of £100,000. It stirred up an administrative controversy which has continued for nearly forty years : was the School to be subject to the Cardiff College Council or a separate constituent College of the University or what was their relation to be ?

On 12 February, 1914 a representative deputation waited on the Chancellor of the Exchequer (Mr. Lloyd George) and appealed to the Government to fulfil the condition attached by Sir William to his gift and provide an adequate maintenance grant. The

Chancellor in effect said ' Yes' provided the School was of a *national* character. An Education Conference followed and it drew up a scheme on national lines which was submitted to the Royal Commission on the Welsh University (1916-1918). In its Final Report (6 February, 1918), the Commission recommended the organisation of the Medical School as a constituent College of the University to be governed under the University by a Council and Senate of its own. I cannot attempt to trace the subsequent negotiations to retain an organic connection between the College and the School or the complicated solution which to-day persists.

The Treasury had early granted permission to Sir William to go ahead with the building of the Physiological block. He had retained in his own hands the choice of architect and contractors. The architect, Colonel Bruce Vaughan, had himself done much to promote the co-operation of the School with the local hospitals. The Colonel's familiar style was Gothic. This meant excluding the new building from Cathays Park on grounds of incongruity with the collegiate buildings already placed on the famous Civic Centre. We tried to have the style changed so that the buildings might be grouped together but in vain ; the donor would not part with his architect and the architect would not part with his style. So the new block found its site on the main thoroughfare.

Such is a brief summary of the early negotiations. There were innumerable deputations, conferences, committees. County Councils threatened to withhold financial support. Eminent consultants were called in and in my Whitehall days I remember advice being sought from Lord Moulton, Dr. Addison, Sir Thomas Lewis, Sir William Osler, Sir Charles Sherrington, Sir Arthur Newsholme and there would be others. An honours student of public administration ought to earn a Ph.D. for an exhaustive study of this example of our Welsh way of life.

Before I leave the Welsh scene I ought perhaps to anticipate future events and make some reference to appointments to College Principalships with which I was in a year or two to be mixed up.

There are four constituent colleges federated into the University of Wales : Aberystwyth, Bangor, Cardiff and Swansea. Each is governed by a court and council and the University itself by court and council. I served as governor and councillor of Aberystwyth and Cardiff and of the University.

The position of Principal at any of the four colleges is held in high popular esteem in Wales. Early in the session 1917-1918 it was understood that the Principal of Cardiff College, Dr. E. H. Griffiths, did not wish to continue in his office beyond that session. Had the Hon. W. N. Bruce, then at the Board of Education, been willing to accept an invitation to succeed him it would almost certainly have been forthcoming. Bruce was the second son of the first Lord Aberdare, and had been under Butler at Harrow and Jowett at Balliol. He knew Wales well and had done much for secondary and university education. He had the finest personal qualities but he was nearly sixty, and deeply rooted in London. Fortunately for Wales he was chosen to succeed Kenyon as Pro-Chancellor of the University and graced the proceedings impartially and with a no less handsome presence.

A committee was appointed to deal with the Cardiff vacancy with Lord Pontypridd as chairman. I knew my name was being mentioned, but I also knew there was nothing like unanimity for me. The Tory Press was unfriendly because of my Labour views and I had annoyed the doctors by supporting medical aid schemes when serving the Insurance Commission. I was not a regular attendant at chapel on Sunday having assumed that editing the *Welsh Outlook* on that day was a sound religious alternative and unconscious of the potency of my bad example. These were deemed sound reasons for opposing me, and there were better ones.   Other and quite outstanding names were being canvassed.   Henry Jones had long been determined—too determined—to run me hard and had been talking to many people and challenging them, as he put it, to drive me out of Wales.   Lord Pontypridd saw him for two hours : " If half the tale of his qualifications were true, he would be the right man, but why isn't the fool religious?"   My old schoolmaster at Pengam wrote, hoping I would return to my Mother's faith.   This led Henry Jones to tell me of a storm which raged around him on the question of eternal punishment in his militant preaching days.   His mother heard of the row and remarked in Welsh : " I am sure, Harry, you were saying some dreadful things."   He replied, "What is the use of your sending me to college for eight years if I am to come back and think exactly like Dafydd y Graig ?" (referring to some half-witted villager).   This seemed completely to satisfy the old lady.

My own inclinations were much more closely interwoven with the college at Aberystwyth.   The Cardiff electors, I thought, would choose a doctor or a scientist in view of possible local developments.

Lloyd-George sometimes suggested that I should stand for Parliament—and his assistance would have been important—but I was not drawn to an M.P.'s life.   Trade Unions preferred to support their own officials rather than university men for parliament, and I was already perhaps too old to learn quickly all the wondrous ways of the House of Commons.   The attraction of the House is that M.P.s are of all sorts, and I would be one of the sorts, but all College Principals are respectable and dignified and I had an innate dislike to being either.   The notion of being a ' Principal ' had a certain ludicrous inappropriateness in my sight.   I was only slowly shedding the unconventionality and intolerance of a rather heterodox and dogmatic early manhood, only slowly and grudgingly, I hope never completely—accepting the wisdom of ' my elders and betters.'

The Cardiff College Council set up an advisory committee of scholars and administrators to suggest suitable names and I was summoned to be inspected by one of them, A. L. Smith, Master of Balliol.

I found the Master in his study apparently making notes for a Bible lesson, as he was poring over a copy of the Bible and scribbling away, bunched up at his desk with his legs in a rug. I occupied myself reading until the gong went for dinner and we joined Mrs. A. L. Smith and two of the seven daughters. The activities of the Food Controller was the main topic of talk. After dinner my host took me aside, got to business and told me Lord Aberdare had written to him about Cardiff. I summarised my history and happened to mention incidentally that I was very glad that I had been sent to work before going to College, and that I wished every university student could have some such experience in a workshop or factory. The Master exclaimed quite excitedly that that was his strong view and that he thought that he alone held it ; he welcomed me into his Church of one member, and quoted the case of his son, a clever student, who had found twelve months in the army an immensely valuable experience. I said that I was not interested in the constitutions, charters, regulations and statutes of universities and would make a very poor Principal in that respect unless I could find some lawyers on whom to devolve the study of them. He recalled Bolingbroke's saying " I am thankful that in the providence of God some men have been called to the work of compiling dictionaries." We had some talk about a scheme of education in citizenship for soldiers. And so to bed. In a few days came a note from the Master : " Thou art the man." Later I learned that of the outside consultants his view was shared by Sir Henry Jones, Sir Henry Hadow and W. N. Bruce.

The list of nominated persons—we were not candidates in a formal sense—was sent to the Senate. Sir Henry Jones, Dr. Isambard Owen, P. E. Matheson and Professor Smithells who had all been nominated were considered to be over-age. The rest were weighed in the academic balance, with insight and fairness so far as I was concerned, and the report went on to the College Council. The Council decided (February 8th) to invite Principal Griffiths to remain on for another year. In the event Trow, Professor of Botany, who had strongly supported me, became acting Principal.

In August, 1919, the Aberystwyth principalship became vacant on the death of T. F. Roberts. Two men were being mentioned as possible successors to Roberts : Professor David Williams and Henry Stuart Jones, the Oxford classical scholar, who was a member of the College Council, and who was to become Principal of the University College of Wales, but not until some years later, 1927-1934. In some ways David Williams would have been admirable. His fine character, his war record, his great public powers would secure the confidence of the fathers and mothers of the students. He would be able to do for the college and for Wales much that the first Principal had done. What his business gifts were I did not know. But I soon learnt that he was marked out to succeed Dr. Owen Prys as head of the Presbyterian Theological College.

I have referred in an earlier volume to the choice of the college registrar, John Humphreys Davies, as the new principal. He was a member of a highly respected Cardiganshire family ; his sister had married Tom Ellis, M.P. ; he was a Presbyterian elder ; a bibliophile and indefatigable collector of Welsh books and ballads and, generally, a most serviceable public figure. His candidature was unexpected and came to my knowledge quite late in the day. I have never concealed my own disappointment and that of my

friends at my failure to be elected. Indeed I probably owe my
defeat to their excessive zeal. One of them, I learnt later, had
prophesied that if appointed, I could be counted on to remove two
or three of the more incompetent professors from the staff ! Nor
was I helped by rumours that my success would produce large contributions to college funds. David Davies, Llandinam, like Henry
Jones, at Cardiff, had been determined, far too determined, to run
me hard and so had another influential councillor, Sir Lleufer
Thomas. Both had underestimated the local influence of the college
president, Sir John Williams, the court physician, himself a bibliophile, who was convinced of the suitability of the registrar for the
higher post. Sir John had long been ill and confined to his house,
but he roused himself to preside at this interview to the dismay of
David Davies.

At the College Council I felt I was before a body of Church
Inquisitors assembled to test my religious beliefs and jealous for
the doctrinal safety of the students. I responded with a vague
unpremeditated confession of idealism, under rather than overstating
my halting undogmatic faith. The person who received the most
paltry treatment at the hands of the Council was the most distinguished candidate on the short list of three—(Sir) John Edward
Lloyd, the national historian, a former student and professor at
Aberystwyth, then professor of History and registrar at Bangor, and
a Fellow of the British Academy. He was given four votes, I got
sixteen, and Davies twenty-three. When the figures were announced,
David Davies lost his temper and burst out of the room. It was a
long time before he was reconciled. J. H. Davies remained principal until his death in 1926.

A month after the Aberystwyth decision the President of the
College at Swansea, Frank Gilbertson, wrote to me : " I want to
know whether you would accept the Principalship of the Swansea
University College if an offer was made you." Two months later

(February 21, 1020) Lord Aberdare, the Cardiff President, wrote from Mountain Ash :

"We have a meeting on Friday to settle the procedure as to the election of a Principal. It is being freely stated that you would neither propose yourself or wish to be proposed. I can quite understand your position if it is so—but if not, I should like to have the honour of proposing you myself."

To these flattering approaches and, much later, to a similar informal sounding from Bangor, I returned polite refusals and I settled down for the next ten years as Deputy Secretary of the Cabinet and then for a further fifteen as Secretary of the Pilgrim Trust.

In retrospect I am glad that all four colleges were spared any experience of my administrative idiosyncracies and heterodox homilies. I easily subdued myself to the anonymous and influential life of a civil servant. In part, no doubt, this was a cowardly retreat into an ivory tower from the rough and tumble of the market place. I made fewer enemies than would have been possible in open conflict, indeed I find it hard to think of any entitled to the epithet.

* * * * * *

At the end of 1916, when we were in the middle of the First World War, a political crisis was blowing up. I was then employed as Secretary of the Welsh National Health Insurance Commission and living in Barry with my wife and three children. Out of the blue I received a telegram summoning me to St. James's Court, London, to see Mr. Lloyd George, where he had a private flat, next door to one occupied by David Davies, with whom I was to stay.

I found Mr. Lloyd George in the thick of the crisis which removed Asquith and landed himself in the premiership on December 7th. In his flat he was able to secure more privacy than at 11, Downing Street, and one of my duties was to keep away unwanted politicians and office seekers. I breakfasted alone with him on

the 9th and had the impertinence to give him some good advice on
how to succeed as Prime Minister. Mr. Lloyd George set up a small
War Cabinet with great speed and planned with Colonel (now Lord)
Hankey a Cabinet Secretariat, the first of its kind in our history.
He told Hankey to find me a place on it and instead of returning
in a few days to the Insurance Commission in Cardiff, I remained
in Whitehall Gardens in the Cabinet Office for 14 years, serving a
succession of Prime Ministers : Lloyd George, Bonar Law, Stanley
Baldwin and Ramsay MacDonald. Sir Percy Watkins took on my
post in Cardiff.

Sometime around 1909 or later I attended a Fabian Summer
School at Llanbedr, Merioneth. I shared rooms with Professors
Tawney and Namier. Sidney and Beatrice Webb, George Lansbury
and many others were there. We were asked out to tea to a new
house which was being extended at Harlech called Wernfawr. A
music room with organ was being added to it. Our host was an
unusual and attractive character, George Davison, who had made
a fortune in Kodak Ltd., and had retired to this residence in Wales.
He lived largely on fruit and nuts and his political views resembled
those of a Tolstoyan anarchist. The architect of the house was
George Walton, and he also had designed the furniture to fit the
rooms. I liked Davison and got to know him well enough to tell
him that such a house on such a wonderful site ought not to be
monopolised by one man or even one family, but should be put to
some public use. I do not claim credit for the fact that he proceeded to adopt a number of children of mal-adjusted ex-cabmen
behind Addison Road, London, about a dozen of them, and brought
them to Harlech where he provided teachers for them. Later he
bought a villa at Cap d'Antibes on the Riviera which had belonged
to the King of the Belgians, and took his big family to a sunnier
clime. Wernfawr was thus free for some social purpose and he

COLEG HARLECH

offered it to me for £25,000. This was beyond my reach and I was also preoccupied with strikes.

When I was at Pengam School I had known a Pontlottyn boy, Henry Gethin Lewis. He had since prospered in business and I turned to him. I asked him to dine in London, I think at the Hotel Cecil, and I brought along to meet him Lord Haldane and Lord Eustace Percy, then Minister of Education. They developed the case for promoting Adult Education and at the end of dinner Henry Lewis handed me an I.O.U. for £7,500, which was the figure to which I had reduced George Davison's price for what is to-day known as Coleg Harlech, a residential college for adult education which opened its doors in 1927 with Ben Bowen Thomas (now Sir Ben) as its first Warden.[1] In its formative years the College enjoyed not only his invaluable constructive guidance but also that of Sir Percy Watkins as Vice-Chairman, Alice Davies as Secretary, W. J. Williams (also of Kodak Ltd) as Treasurer and Miss Nellie Williams, its House Mistress—to name only its chief officers and none of its many benefactors. I say nothing of the zeal of many who helped then and in the years that followed. I'll make one exception in favour of a friend whom I met in an odd way.

Henry Yates Thompson (1838-1928) had been a head-boy at Harrow in Palmerston's time, and one of his life's ambitions had been to collect the hundred finest illuminated manuscripts in the world. This he did. His plan had been never to buy any additional

---

[1] Newbattle Abbey, formerly in the possession of Philip Kerr, Lord Lothian, and now a residential college for adult education, may be regarded as the offspring of Coleg Harlech. It was a visit which Lothian paid to Harlech which led him in 1936 to devote Newbattle to the service of adult education in Scotland. It was opened in January 1937 with the help of educational trust funds and private benefactors of whom Philip Kerr was himself one. The War of 1939-1945 diverted its use and it was only in the autumn of 1950 that it was restored with Dr. Edwin Muir as its new Warden to carry on the work of its first Warden, Alexander Fraser.

volume unless it was decidedly superior in value and interest to one at least of his original hundred and upon its acquisition pitilessly to discard the least fascinating of the said hundred. Then he decided to sell or give away the 100 hoping they would go " aux héritiers de mes gouts." Three sales took place at Sotheby's in 1919, 1920, and 1921 and the total raised was around £144,000. Among the items sold on March 23rd, 1920, was Lot XXIX *Sarum Missal of the Sherbrooke Family*—so called because it had been in the possession of that family from the 16th century. More recently it had belonged to William Morris. It was on vellum decorated with initials in gold and colour, with branches extending up and down the margins. Lot XLII was the *De Grey Horae*, an English Book of Hours of the first half of the fifteen century, also on vellum. Thompson bought it from Quaritch in 1895. These two MSS. were bought by Hugh Blaker for Gregynog. I was asked by the Misses Davies, the new owners, to take temporary charge of them as they were going abroad. I put them in a safe in which the Cabinet Minutes were kept at 2 Whitehall Gardens and here months after they were found to his astonishment by my colleague, Sir John Chancellor, a relative of Yates Thompson. The result was an invitation to luncheon to meet the famous collector and his wife at 19, Portman Square. In 1878, he had married Elizabeth Alexandra Murray, the eldest and remarkable daughter of a remarkable father, George Smith of Smith, Elder and Co., the merchant prince and publisher, the friend of Charlotte Bronte, Mrs. Gaskell, Thackeray, Browning, of half the famous authors of the Victorian Age, the founder of the Dictionary of National Biography whose heirs and executors donated it to the University of Oxford.

At this house I met scholars and statesmen, bibliographical experts and delightful American women of whom I remember Mrs. Andrew Carnegie, Elizabeth Robins and Ruth Draper. But above all I met our hostess full of grace and wit and truth. Ruth Draper told me that E.A.M.T.—Aunt Dolly to her intimates—and three or four similar Grand Old Ladies of England, the like of whom were not easily found in the New World, attracted her to this country rather than her professional engagements. The first night I dined at 19, Portman Square I was shown the manuscript of *Jane Eyre* and it was only one of many treasures I was to inspect and enjoy in twenty years of friendship. Mrs. Yates Thompson was crippled by arthritis and propelled herself about the house in a bath chair. It made little difference to her gaiety and exquisite hospitality. She never betrayed fatigue or indifference to a guest and her criticism of a book or picture or poem or person might be pungent but it would not be bitter. There was no protective fuss made of the household treasures. She not only admired beautiful books as a connoisseur, she read them. A herd of Jersey cows was only one of her hobbies, libraries was another. She it was who gave me courage to build the library at Coleg Harlech and provided unasked about a fourth of its cost. To the cricketers of Harrow School she was a fairy God-mother but of that and much else I only learnt from the memorial tribute paid by Elizabeth Robins in *Portrait of a Lady*. She continued her husband's taboos after his death and when I went to bed at Oving, their country house near Aylesbury, it was by candle-light. Telephones and motor cars were banned from both houses. Instead she would accompany me in her open carriage after luncheon from Portman Square through the Park or Regent Street to the office of the Pilgrim Trust in the Adelphi. I felt I was riding beside a Queen, and so I was.

* * * * * * *

"It is very meet, right, and our bounden duty that we should at all times and in all places give thanks." I want to close this little book on that note. Ingratitude, we are elsewhere told, is a great-sized monster. For my scraps of good deeds I have been accorded most generous recognition all through the years.

In 1928 the University of Wales conferred on me the honorary degree of Doctor of Laws, and in 1947 the University of St. Andrews did me a like honour. Glasgow had set a precedent in 1922 and on that occasion my Welsh friends loaded me with gifts : the robes, a Rothenstein drawing, a grand piano. These unsought tributes to general usefulness from academic bodies have a great attraction for a person who is no scholar, in the technical sense. Rhymney in 1939 gave me a Barnsley bookcase which holds Gregynog books and many others 'from the author'. To this presentation in Brynhyfryd Chapel with troops of friends, came two Companions of Honour, Violet Markham and Philip Kerr (Lord Lothian) and many letters which I treasure. In 1938 friends of Coleg Harlech presented me with a volume of essays, *Harlech Studies*, specially written by tutors and students ; in 1942 more friends presented the College with my portrait painted by Murray Urquhart. In 1945 the Cymmrodorion Society awarded me their medal. The climax of native good-will was reached, in the same year, when I was invited to become President of my old college at Aberystwyth. I was then seventy-five and my rôle ornamental. I preside over an indulgent Court and Council, am kept on the rails by extremely efficient official guides, and am diplomatically excused speechmaking so that I may not put " both feet in it".

That was five years ago and in the meantime I have busied my-self with tracing in outline the career of David Lloyd George at the invitation of the Harvard University Press for a volume in its series *Makers of Modern Europe*. I was rather old to attempt this task, one which, as Lord Baldwin said, could only be discharged, if at all, by ten men. To quote the biblical text which decorated his bedroom, Lloyd George pursued " a path which no fowl knoweth and which the vulture's eye hath not seen." It was hardly to be expected that my sight could succeed where these birds had failed. My life has been much enriched in this last decade by my association with the *Observer*, organized as a Trust, and with its remarkable editors, Ivor Brown and David Astor. My eightieth birthday was celebrated by a gathering of fifty friends in the Peers' Dining Room, Houses of Parliament. Sir Wilfred Eady presided, Mr. Attlee sent his blessing, Right and Left were represented. Lady Astor was there and Professor Tawney and the headmasters of such different schools as Winchester and Gordonstoun, Walter Oakeshott and Kurt Hahn. I was delighted with the presence of sons and daughters of the four Prime Ministers I had tried to serve : Lady Megan Lloyd-George, M.P., Richard Law, M.P., Windham Baldwin and Sheila MacDonald (now Mrs. Lochhead). Finally, I have occupied myself with these, I hope, harmless recollections of half a lifetime spent chiefly in Scotland, Ireland and Wales. How far I have enough energy and discretion left to select and publish some account of the second half, spent in England, remains to be seen.

A final word to any young student who may read these pages and wish me to compress into a paragraph the lessons of a long life. They are all commonplaces. The supreme blessing is the love of a good woman ; the next best is the friendship of half a dozen. Communism, Socialism, Fascism, Nationalism are transient aspects of the human struggle. Universal education is enormously worth while striving for, but it will not solve our problems, not if all students take Firsts and all become Professors. Happiness is a by-product, do not chase it. Place others first and self second is a golden rule. To be merry you do not need to be flown with wine, nor is a night-club a sure refuge from misery. Rest and toil, joy and pain, beauty and ashes—these are and always have been everywhere the stuff of life, the warp and woof of its good and evil. We mingle the elements variously in the vale of soul-making, or, if you prefer in the work-shop of character-building.   If you live long enough, or are pre-maturely wise, you should reach the other side of disillusion without bitterness or cynicism, indeed with serenity if your faith can reach beyond the badness of man to the ultimate goodness of God.

* * * * * * *

The delay in printing this book, due to the scarcity of paper, enables me to add a postscript as it goes to press.

I have hardly mentioned Gregynog in the preceding pages. My debt to that gracious House is not easily or briefly recorded. To-day I have been there for the hundredth time.   The home of Gwendoline and Margaret Davies is unique among country houses in Wales and I know no parallel in England.   There are Glyndebourne with its music, Cliveden with its politics, others with their sporting and week-end bridge parties.   The story of Hafod has recently been told by Elizabeth Inglis Jones and someday the story of Gregynog will be written—its gardens, its music, its pictures, its Press, all of great beauty, all in widest commonalty spread.

There were weeks when the house was socialized, if not nation-alized, an example of civilized living.   Notables came from London seeking its rest and peace : Lord and Lady Baldwin, Lord and Lady Macmillan, G.B.S. and Charlotte.   There were weeks of festival. A small domestic choir, after months of intensive training by W. R. Allen, was led by Walford Davies or Adrian Boult in such master-pieces as the St. Matthew Passion, the Grecian Urn, the Music-Makers.   The finest string players accompanied.   Charles Clements, Elsie Suddaby and Keith Falkner came often.   Poetry had its equal place and Lascelles Abercrombie and Helen Waddell read to us.

Conferences of social workers gathered from the coal valleys of South Wales whence flowed the family fortune ; earnest groups dis-cussed adult education, world-peace, the League of Nations. Forty guests might stay in the house and scores of neighbours would be invited to the music-making. Gwen Davies and Dora Herbert Jones drew up an Order of Service for Sunday morning worship, the devotional essence of the liturgies of all the Churches, and the Press would print it finely. All was free.

I have just returned from a Memorial Service to the chief creator and inspirer of this splendid hospitality—a shy, timid, modest religious spirit, Gwendoline Elizabeth Davies, who died at Oxford on July 3rd.

Today over two hundred of her friends assembled in the music-room, ablaze with flowers, to join in a Service in the Gregynog tradition. With the help of Bach and Beethoven, Bunyan and Henry Vaughan, we thanked God for her :

" For her courage and sincerity ; for her nurture of the Arts, for her love and service of the beautiful, and for our memories of her in this room ; for her constant remembrance of the sick and suffering ; for her generous and unfailing interest in the work of the Church at home and overseas ; and for her great love for humanity."

Aberystwyth
September 7th, 1951

INDEX OF NAMES

171

WARE, Sir Fabian, 70.
WATKINS, Sir Percy, 129, 135, 137-139, 141, 162, 163.
WATT, James, 7, 66.
WAXWEILER, Professor, 150.
WEBB, Beatrice, 30n, 37n, 71-73, 162.
WEBB, Sydney, 27, 29, 71, 72-73, 162.
WEERT, M. de, 152.
WEDMORE, Frederick, 140.
WEIR, Lord, 41.
WELSH, Freddie, 134.
WESTON, Agnes, 65.
WHEATLEY, John, 41.
WHELDON, P. J., 125.
WHISTLER, 140.
WHITE, Mrs. Eirene, 120.
WIESER, Friederich von, 19, 22.
WILDE, Jimmy, 134.
WILDE, Oscar, 63.
WILLIAMS, Dr. Daniel, 4, 5, 6.
WILLIAMS, Professor David (later Principal, Theological College), 159.

WILLIAMS, David (Professor of Welsh History), 143n.
WILLIAMS, Dr. D. Llewelyn, 136.
WILLIAMS, Professor Lloyd, 145.
WILLIAMS, Sir John, 65, 66-68, 125, 160.
WILLIAMS, Margaret Lindsay, 144.
WILLIAMS, Nellie, 163.
WILLIAMS, R. R., 5, 11, 12, 60, 73, 78.
WILLIAMS, Judge Vaughan, 67.
WILLIAMS, W. J. (Ministry of Education), 141.
WILLIAMS, W. J. (Kodak Ltd.), 163.
WILSON, Professor James, 93, 94.
WILSON, Richard, 140, 153.
WORKMAN, Frank, 119.
WRIGHT, Willie, 30.
WYNDHAM, George, 103, 104.

YEATS, J. B., 91, 99.
YEATS, W. B., 113, 139.

ZAMENHOF, Dr., 74.